Living me to we

The Guide for Socially Conscious Canadians

CRAIG KIELBURGER | MARC KIELBURGER

Research by Laura Trethewey

Me to We
225 Carlton Street
Toronto ON
Canada M5A 2L2
www.metowe.com/books

Distributed by
Greystone Books, D&M Publishers Inc.

Cataloguing in Publication data available from Library and Archives Canada
ISBN: 978-0-9784375-6-5 (p-book)
ISBN: 978-0-9784375-5-8 (e-book)

Printed and bound in China
Text printed on 100% post-consumer, acid-free paper

Book design by Frances Data
Illustrations by TurnStyle Imaging
Research by Laura Trethewey

MIX
Paper
FSC FSC® C008047

Living me to we

The Guide for Socially Conscious Canadians

Contents

78

102

138

130

134

Introduction

WHAT DOES IT MEAN TO LIVE *ME* TO *WE*? You might have worn a Me to We T-shirt or bracelet, read a Me to We book or gone on a Me to We trip – but living *me* to *we* – is a journey towards leading a positive daily legacy.

When you drill down to the hard numbers, Canadians donate less than one percent of their income. But that statistic doesn't tell the whole story. What about the shovelling of an older neighbour's driveway, or the chicken soup you delivered for a sick friend? What we do to make the world a better place – without the hint of a tax credit or thanks in return – is living *me* to *we*. As the great social historian Howard Zinn wrote, "Small acts, when multiplied by millions of people, can transform the world." This is our guide to helping you turn these small, everyday acts into universal change.

Through our work with the charity Free The Children, we've visited a combined total of 55 countries. And, with over 2,000 Free The Children groups across Canada, we know the passion of young people and mentors here at home. Believe us when we say: we Canadians won the lottery when it comes to nationality. Craig will extol the beauty of St. John's, Newfoundland (the craggy cliffs, the steely expanse of the sea!) and Marc will do the same for Manitoban women (he married one from St. Boniface!). In short, we love our country. Through our journeys, we've come to learn that Canada is much more than hockey and Timbits. What makes this country the greatest place to live in the world is our compassion, friendliness and willingness to roll-up our sleeves to help. With all the gifts our country has, from poutine to politeness, we're uniquely positioned to make the world a little better, too.

We started by seeking out notable Canadians whose examples of living *me* to *we* inspired us. We asked Margaret Atwood about how she reduces her carbon footprint with the trusty aide of her LongPen (pg. 34) and asked Rick Hansen about keeping his connection to nature and family (pg. 94). We also spoke with many Canadians whose names you might not know. Meet Meghan, who adopted a cat from the hard streets of Vancouver's downtown east side (pg. 138) to the Girouard family who take staycations and use public transit to rediscover their hometown (pg. 82). And, slowly but surely, we created a guide of 50 world-changing acts.

The tips contained here are far from exhaustive. Instead, this is a starting point as well as a challenge to get out there and change the world using these tips and your own. We need your help to finish the story. Small acts can change the world and it starts with you.

Live the Change!

Craig Kielburger   Marc Kielburger

YOUR ROADMAP

Living Me to We will take you through a day in the life of a socially conscious Canadian. Here's how!

Take a closer look at a part of your day with this food for thought.

Check out these solid tips for making a change, big or small.

These handy clocks will guide you through your day of living *me* to *we*!

Get more in-depth information here.

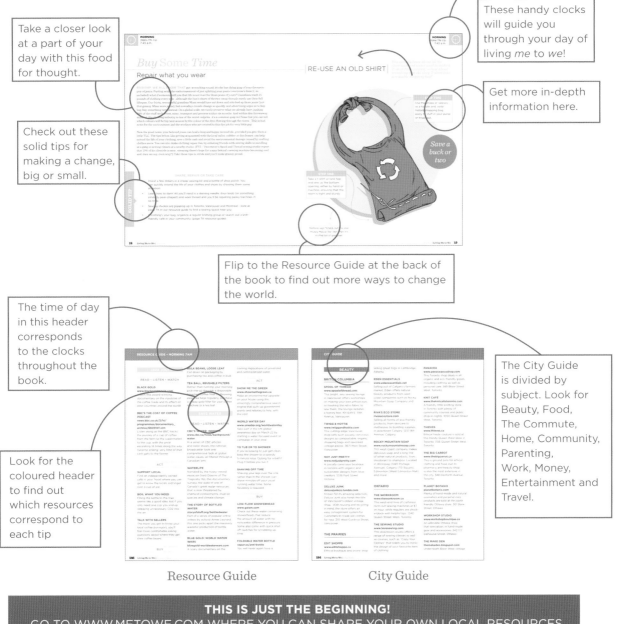

Flip to the Resource Guide at the back of the book to find out more ways to change the world.

The time of day in this header corresponds to the clocks throughout the book.

Look for the coloured header to find out which resources correspond to each tip

The City Guide is divided by subject. Look for Beauty, Food, The Commute, Home, Community, Parenting, Work, Money, Entertainment and Travel.

Resource Guide

City Guide

THIS IS JUST THE BEGINNING!
GO TO WWW.METOWE.COM WHERE YOU CAN SHARE YOUR OWN LOCAL RESOURCES AND TIPS. JOIN WITH OTHER SOCIALLY CONSCIOUS CANADIANS.

Morning
WAKE ME UP

Java *Jolt*

Make Your Cuppa Count

DOES A CUP OF FAIR-TRADE COFFEE taste better than the conventional stuff? In a taste-test showdown, we bet only the finest coffee connoisseurs can tell. But it's where your espresso comes from that could leave a bad taste in your mouth.

At the beginning of the coffee-picking season in Ecuador – one of the biggest coffee exporters in the world – we drove along a dirt road edged by plantations. We pulled over to take a look at the coffee cherries hanging from the trees and caught sight of a group of pickers. There were whole families of transient workers, dragging with them the day's harvest in brown burlap sacks. Some were kids, not even taller than the sacks that hung from their necks. As we chatted, a truck pulled up and a farmhand called out for the workers to take their bags to the weighing station where the day's wages were paid out based on bulk. A picker muttered that the scale was crooked. The farmhand yelled back that the pickers were the thieves, tipping the scales with metal hidden in the bags. As a blistering sun beat down and the argument heated up, we looked on, understanding only the worried looks on every face.

Later, we visited a fair-trade cooperative of family-owned farms. There were no kids running around. One farmer proudly told us they were in school. That evening, we sat with other co-op members, sipping the fruits of their labour. A feeling of excitement filled the air as they discussed buying new books for the school and a water cistern with their fair wages. Here, the future wasn't something to be feared. It was embraced.

In the Canadian cafés where we grab our skim lattes or double grandes, those scenes feel far away from us, especially with the music and conversation and coffee percolating in the background. The hot drink in our hands comes to us with a dark track record; coffee beans are the second most traded product in the world after oil. It's impossible to ask for fair trade at the gas station, so instead we can take advantage of what's on offer behind many local coffee counters. It always keeps us connected to the farmers down south.

A GOOD BREW

- If you're often forgetting your flower-decaled thermos on your desk, buy a few and keep them at key coffee-fetching points throughout your day: in your car, at your desk and in your backpack.
- Keep a bag of fair-trade beans at your desk so you can make your own fair-trade brew cheaply whenever you can.
- Share the wealth: buy a bag of fair-trade beans for a co-worker, friend or family member.
- Ask for fair-trade wherever you can: choose fair-trade chocolate, sugar, flowers, honey, gold, rice, spices, herbs, tea and bananas.
- Buy fair-trade chocolate for Easter, Christmas, Hannukah or Halloween.
- Buy a fair-trade soccer ball for a child's birthday.

SOLID TIP

WHAT YOUR CAFFEINE FIX COSTS

KNOW YOUR COFFEE

There's a litany of labels to decipher on your bag of beans. Here's what those signs really mean:

FAIR TRADE CERTIFIED
These beans are farmed small-scale and producers are audited for sustainability and labour standards.

CERTIFIED ORGANIC
Everything you've come to expect of the organic label (no chemicals and sustainable farming practices).

RAINFOREST ALLIANCE CERTIFIED
Make sure your latte doesn't plow up an untouched rainforest to make way for a massive cost-effective plantation with this label that protects the natural, lush coffee-growing habitat as well as ensuring sustainability, labour standards and education.

20% LABOUR - BARISTA

17% RENT

18% COFFEE*

7-8% PAPER CUP AND LID

5-8% DAIRY

5-7% SUGAR

24.5% OTHER

COSTS INCLUDE:
planting, harvesting, exporting, shipping and importing

- Only a *fraction* of your $2 cup reaches a coffee farmer far away.

GO TO PAGE 152 FOR MORE TIPS AND INFORMATION

Source: 2005 Study, Coffee Association of Canada, adjusted for higher coffee prices.

Flushed Away

Conserve Water

WHERE ELSE IN THE WORLD do people flood their backyards every winter day to make a hockey rink? We're a nation of water wasters, but our hockey-loving habits can be eco-friendly, too. When we visited a reserve in Manitoba, we saw the difference in living. In many such communities, people live precariously boiling water or drinking bottled H_2O. Some said the tap water was too dirty even to bathe in. We think of Canada as a world-class country, but half a million Aboriginal Canadians go without access to safe water.

Now compare that to the rest of the country, which uses an astonishing amount of water (an estimated 343 litres per day on average) all available with the easy turn of a tap. Only Americans use more water. We use and abuse most of this water in our bathrooms. There is nothing like a hot, relaxing bath on a cold winter morning, and afternoon and evening and ... you get the point. We love baths and showers. In fact, over 65 percent of the water used at home is sucked down the bathroom drain.

We've tried to cut our watery ways by speeding up the sudsy soak. But there are better ways to reduce than jumping out with soap still behind our ears. Older toilet models can use as much as 20 litres per flush – approximately the size of a water cooler jug! Ditch that H_2O guzzler for a new and improved edition (some flush close to half a litre of water), which most provinces and municipalities will cover up to $150. That beloved shower streams 15 to 20 litres a minute straight down the drain. A low-flow showerhead halves that amount with no noticeable difference in water pressure. Some models come with an easy shut-off button for sudsing. Knowing that you're not wasting water in the washroom? Now that's relaxing...

WATER WISE

GARDEN:
- Plant indigenous plants that need no watering.
- Make sure to water your lawn at dawn or dusk; the yard will evaporate less water and stay moist longer.
- Avoid overwatering: a typical lawn requires only one water every four to five days.

KITCHEN:
- As if you needed another reason to load up the ol' washer and call it a day, now studies say we conserve more water with a dishwasher than handwashing.
- Promise to never throw away water; pour leftover water on plants instead.
- Keep your drinking water cold in the fridge, rather than running the faucet until it's cold.
- Thaw frozen food overnight, rather than running under hot water.

BATHROOM:
- Turn off the tap while brushing teeth.
- Troubleshoot your tank. Put a few drops of food colouring in the tank, wait a minute and see if the colour seeps into the bowl. If so, you've sprung a leak, matey!
- Place a 2-litre bottle in your tank to displace the water, making sure it doesn't interfere with the pulleys and traps of the tank.

SOLID TIP

WHERE THE H$_2$O GOES | *Indoor Water Use*

COOKING, DRINKING & CLEANING
15%

WASHING MACHINE
20%

SHOWER & BATH
35%

TOILET
30%

GO TO PAGE 152 FOR MORE TIPS AND INFORMATION
Source: *David Suzuki's Green Guide* (David Suzuki Foundation).

Clothes Minded

Wear What Matters

RANSACKING YOUR CLOSET to unearth an outfit often leads to the same conclusion: I have nothing to wear! (Yes, guys think it too, ladies.) But more likely, we have nothing ethical to wear. Prices have plunged faster than V-necks on men. This means we're buying a third more clothing than just a few years ago. All this fast fashion is bad for the environment (cotton is often doused with pesticides like it's cheap cologne) and bad for the people in distant sweatshops. After seeing the factories where these here-today-gone-tomorrow togs are made, it's impossible to feel good about what we're wearing.

Me to We Style says good-bye to guilt-ridden clothing. With the help of co-founder Oliver Madison, we launched a company that doesn't rely on pesticide-coated cotton or children in sweatshops, or create untold amounts of pollution and environmental damage. To put that in fashion speak: that is SO last season! So few clothing companies follow ethical standards that Me to We Style had to set its own. We use organic and sweatshop-free fabrics, recycled polyester from plastic bottles – all manufactured in Canada. If that's not enough, for every T-shirt sold, we also plant a tree, and half our profits go to our charity partner, Free The Children. A wardrobe that builds schools, digs wells and makes the world a better place. That doesn't just solve your what-to-wear dilemma, it makes a real fashion statement.

PAIN IS NOT BEAUTY

SOLID TIP

- Cut back on your closet! Save your cash for that extra special, ethically made something-something.
- Look for clothing companies, such as Patagonia, Icebreaker, Me to We Style, that account for its entire supply chain from start to finish.
- Remember sustainable, ethical clothing is often better made, lasts longer and saves you money.
- Shop vintage or second-hand for a true recycled fashion experience.
- Take note: not all designer or expensive clothing is ethically made. Checking websites, asking in-store or running a quick search online will turn up more answers.
- Check out local and hand-made products at craft festivals or online marketplaces, such as Etsy.

THE LIFE OF A T-SHIRT

- (3) **North America** — Printed, Sold
- (5) **Japan** — High End Vintage
- **China** — (2) Milled, Woven, Cut, Assembled
- (1) **U.S.** — Cotton
- **Africa** — (4) Cast-offs

U.S. – Cotton
Farmed in the U.S., subsidized cotton drives down profits for producers from the other 70 cotton-producing countries in the world.

China – Milled, Woven, Cut, Assembled
The largest exporter of clothing, where reports state that workers can make as little as 12 to 18 cents per hour, often in unsafe conditions.

North America – Printed, Sold
The T-shirts end up in stores around the country, sold for as little as $5 a pop.

Africa – Cast-offs
Over the last decade, second-hand clothing charities have reported a 67% increase in donations. Africa gets the dregs of this system: cheap clothing is packed into mass bundles and sold at markets across the continent.

Japan - High End Vintage
Wondering where grandma's fur coat ended up? Japan is the largest buyer of vintage and high-end donated clothing.

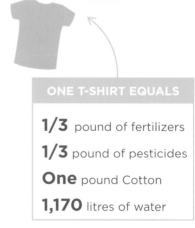

ONE T-SHIRT EQUALS

1/3 pound of fertilizers

1/3 pound of pesticides

One pound Cotton

1,170 litres of water

GO TO PAGE 153 FOR MORE TIPS AND INFORMATION

Source: "Waste Couture: Environmental Impact of the Clothing Industry," *Environmental Health Perspectives*, September 2007.

My Chemical Romance

Cosmetics' Ugly Secret

WORKING AT A NON-PROFIT where the majority of the staff is female, we're surrounded by women all day. Most gravitate to the natural side of the perfume spectrum (and hey, that side looks great, too!) but on occasion a woman will pass us in the hallway, travelling in this perfume-scented bubble. Our first thought is usually "how can she smell exactly like morning dew?" But our second is usually one of concern. Every morning the average woman spritzes and dabs 12 personal care products on her face and body, exposing her to 126 different chemicals, some of them carcinogens, hormone disruptors and neurotoxins. We dudes don't fare much better: the equation works out to eight personal care products and 86 different chemicals. We have no trouble reducing our "beauty" routine – Craig's only consists of that dubious crystal deodorant anyways. We may be your typical guys, but we're also loud and proud feminists. After considering the dubious chemical profile of so many cosmetics, we figured there had to be a way for the gals (and guys) in our lives to pamper themselves safely.

So, we compiled a list of companies that care about our bodies and searched the kitchen cabinets for one-step primping products. We took tips from sources in the know, like eco-minded starlet Rachel McAdams' blog. Check out the suggestions below and our resource guide for the fruits of our labour. Plus, now we understand the importance of the perfect moisturizer, shampoo or deodorant better than ever before. It's not only about choosing a product that makes you look great, but also one that does us no harm. Whether that's a homemade face scrub or a new local, chemical-free beauty company, there are plenty of ways to create a tried-and-true beauty regimen – minus the chemicals.

SHOP, BREW AND CONSERVE

- Tell your beloved but sinful cosmetic company it's not okay to use sketchy ingredients.

- Read before you buy. If you can't pronounce an ingredient name or have no idea what it means, hold off and research first.

- Beware of terms that seem gentler, but have no standards to prove it, such as hypoallergenic, allergy-tested, fragrance-free and dermatologist-tested.

- Is that green do-gooding company the real deal? Bleach company Clorox bought out Burt's Bees, Colgate-Palmolive has Tom's of Maine and L'Oreal has The Body Shop. Will formerly small, sustainable companies influence big-company practices or vice versa? The jury's still out, so keep an eye on the ingredient list.

- Ever read the instructions for your products? We thought not. Most recommend using only a small amount rather than a massive dollop. Less product washed down drains and into waterways means your bottle lasts longer, too.

- Support local companies that prove they care about your health.

SOLID TIP

ONE STEP BEAUTY

The average North American splurges on personal care products every year – over $600 per year! Turn to your kitchen cupboard instead where a few universal foodstuffs can pamper as well as nourish.

CORN STARCH

Wake up in the morning with an oily head of hair, but have no time for a shower?

A sprinkle of corn starch – a natural dry shampoo – on your roots solves this dilemma, sucking up the oil fast.

BAKING SODA

No need for fancy exploding bath bombs. A half-cup of plain old baking soda in your soak leaves your skin silky smooth.

COCONUT OIL

At room temperature, coconut oil stays solid and works as a moisturizer for your face and body, as well as an eye make-up remover.

THE TOP THREE NASTIES

Many industrial chemicals crop up in our toiletry bags to make products cheaper, last longer or smell nicer. Canada is not as bad as the U.S. (Health Canada has banned 500 ingredients; the FDA only 8), but these three could still be clogging your pores.

- **Parabens:** A preservative that keeps out fungi and other bacteria has also surfaced in worrisome places such as breast cancer tissue.

- **Phthalates:** A plasticizer that crops up in 80% of mainstream cosmetics and is linked to speeding up puberty in young girls and reproductive disorders in women.

- **Formaldehyde:** Remember those glowing jars of preserved body parts in *Frankenstein* movies? Yup, formaldehyde is the same stuff and it is not required on an ingredient list when it's created in the manufacturing process. That's scarier than any horror movie we know.

GO TO PAGE 153 FOR MORE TIPS AND INFORMATION
Source: *Green Beauty Guide*, The Campaign for Safe Cosmetics, and Femme Toxic.

Buy Some *Time*

Repair What You Wear

RIIIIIIIIIIP. WE ALL KNOW THAT GUT-WRENCHING SOUND: it's the last dying gasp of your favourite pair of jeans. Putting aside the embarrassment of just splitting your pants (everyone's done it, us included), what if someone told you that life is not over for those jeans of yours? Canadians trash 15 pounds of clothing every year, although the lion's share of thrown-away threads rarely use their full lifespan. Our feisty, resourceful Grandma Mimi would have sat down and stitched up those jeans (not that Granny Mimi wore jeans), but nowadays trends change so quickly and advertising urges us to buy, buy, buy something new instead. On a global scale, we rarely preserve what we already have, junking 99 percent of the stuff we harvest, mine, transport and process within six months. And within this throwaway mindset, the clothing industry is one of the worst culprits; it's a common quip in China that you can tell which colours will be hip next season by the colour of the dyes flowing through the rivers. This is bad news for the environment and the workers who receive very little pay.

Now the good news: your beloved jeans can lead a long and happy second life, provided you give them a little TLC. The tips below, like getting acquainted with the local tailor, cobbler or drycleaner, can help extend the life of your clothing, save a little cash and avoid the environmental damage caused by crafting clothes anew. You can also make clothing repair fun, by enlisting friends with sewing skills or enrolling as a gang in sewing classes at a nearby studio. (Vancouver's Spool and Thread sewing studio reports that 10 percent of its clientele is men, meaning there's hope for a man behind a sewing machine becoming cool and, dare we say, even sexy?) Take these tips in stride and you'll make granny proud.

SHARE, REPAIR OR TAKE CARE

SOLID TIP

- Invest a few dollars in a cheap sewing kit and a bottle of shoe polish. You can quickly extend the life of your clothes and shoes by showing them some attention.

- Learn how to darn! All you'll need is a darning needle, door knob (or something similarly pear-shaped) and wool thread and you'll be repairing pesky toe holes in no time.

- Sewing studios are popping up in Toronto, Vancouver and Montreal. Check the resource guide to find a sewing space near you.

- If knitting is your thing, organize a regular knitting group or search out a knit-friendly café in your community.

RE-USE AN OLD SHIRT

You already know about all the chemicals and water used to make a T-shirt from scratch, so how about remaking that old sleeping shirt into a reusable shopping bag?

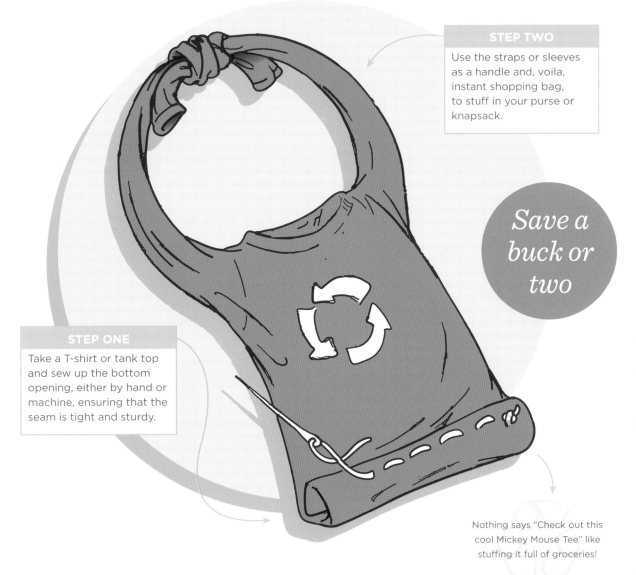

STEP TWO

Use the straps or sleeves as a handle and, voila, instant shopping bag, to stuff in your purse or knapsack.

Save a buck or two

STEP ONE

Take a T-shirt or tank top and sew up the bottom opening, either by hand or machine, ensuring that the seam is tight and sturdy.

Nothing says "Check out this cool Mickey Mouse Tee" like stuffing it full of groceries!

GO TO PAGE 154 FOR MORE TIPS AND INFORMATION

USE WHAT YOU GOT

The Buried Life

Meet Duncan, Johnnie, Ben and Dave, the four childhood-buds-turned-superstars of MTV's *The Buried Life*. Growing up in Victoria, British Columbia these boys were taught to reuse and repurpose whatever they had. Back then it wasn't called "socially conscious living" – just life.

THE MOMENT: "None of us were pampered growing up," says Ben. "So, we learned to be resourceful. I was almost shocked by what my mom would do. She never threw away Christmas wrapping paper. Never. So, we'd be wrapping presents in the same paper for 10 years." Brothers Johnnie and Duncan remember that food waste didn't exist in their house: "Our mom made one big meal on Monday. Whatever wasn't finished would go into a new meal on Tuesday and then whatever wasn't finished that night went into a new meal on Wednesday. Everything was used."

THE MISSION: From B.C. to L.A., the life-time pals made a big jump when they moved south for the small screen. "Growing up on the West Coast, we all have an appreciation for the outdoors and the environment. The differences between Victoria and Los Angeles hit us the most when we saw that recycling doesn't happen much here," says Ben. "I was always impressed by Steve Nash, who's from our hometown. He moved to Dallas where they don't have a recycling program and set one up in the schools there. That's what we want to do: lead by example when we can."

THE HABIT: Day to day, *The Buried Life* stars try to keep connected to their roots in Victoria. Either they're driving across the country in a repurposed purple bus called Penelope, or skateboarding across town wearing second-hand clothing. Even the bunk bed sheets on Penelope are passed down from Dave and his brothers. It's a nice blast from the past, as each bed is outfitted with sheets of each cast member's childhood heroes and hobbies. (Johnnie has Hercules, Duncun has He-Man, Dave has Smurfs and Ben has planets.) "You can take the guys out of Canada, but you can't take the Canada out of the guys" is their motto.

THE BURIED LIFE HANGING
OUT ON LOCATION.

*"But often, in the world's most crowded streets,
But often, in the din of strife,
There rises an unspeakable desire
After the knowledge of our **buried life.**"*

MATTHEW ARNOLD

Morning
BEFORE
YOU
GO GO

2:00 a.m
3:00 a.m
4:00 a.m
5:00 a.m
6:00 a.m
7:00 a.m
8:00 a.m
9:00 a.m
10:00 a.m
11:00 a.m
12:00 p.m
1:00 p.m
2:00 p.m
3:00 p.m
4:00 p.m
5:00 p.m
6:0

00 p.m

9:00 p.m
10:00 p.m
11:00 p.m
12:00 a.m

The *Omnivore's* Way

Eat Less Meat

SOME PEOPLE TELL STORIES OF HORRIBLE DATES. Us? We can regale you with tales of woe about going vegetarian. Like the times we burnt that lentil chili or singed the barbequed tempeh and had dinner guests sneaking bits into their napkins. Or the countless times Craig's resolve has crumbled, after back-to-back overseas flights, where the vegetarian option consists of cold tofu and mystery sauce or the meat-free airport offering is white bread and cheese. And then there is that tiny crustacean, the shrimp, which keeps tempting us away from the vegetarian lifestyle, but harvesting shrimp creates serious environmental damage to our ocean floors. We could go on, but we'll spare you.

Eating meat packs a powerful punch to the environment and our health. Our carnivorous ways far outweigh the pollution caused by driving – one kilo of beef equals 20 kg of pollution-causing emissions – but we doubt that chowing down on steak 'n' eggs will ever attract the same derision as, say, driving an SUV. Meat tastes too good, even though in excess, it's bad for us. A meat-heavy diet boosts our cholesterol and chances of heart disease, cancer and diabetes. A U.K. study estimated that trimming meat to just three meals a week could save the nation 45,000 lives and over $1 billion in health care costs every year. And yet, after all the very good arguments for going vegan or vegetarian, only 4 percent of Canadians do so. There has to be a better, more guilt-free solution to minimizing meat consumption. You can become a part-time vegetarian or follow the Meatless Monday trend or the "vegan-before-six" approach. Or simply evaluate your diet and figure out what works best for you on the path to the good life.

SOCIALLY CONSCIOUS CUISINE

- Hey meat-lover! Try turning meat into the supporting player of your meal, rather than the main attraction, such as a massive salad with a side of grilled fish or a veggie stir-fry with tofu and chicken.

- Fake meat has come a long way: try the fake duck à l'orange or tempeh pate. It might not taste like the real thing; it might taste a whole lot better!

- Try the veggie option on the menu at your next meal out.

- Pick up a vegetarian cookbook from the library.

- Host a vegetarian- or vegan-friendly potluck and see what your friends cook up.

- Have a vegetarian or vegan pal? Ask for favourite recipes, tips and tricks for upping vegetable and bean protein every day.

- The key to vegetarian delight is in the sauce. From Thai and Indian curries to Italian pesto, simple tamari or black bean sauce — all can be found in the grocery store aisle near you.

SOLID TIP

WHAT'S THE BEEF?

The meat on your plate has serious environmental costs.

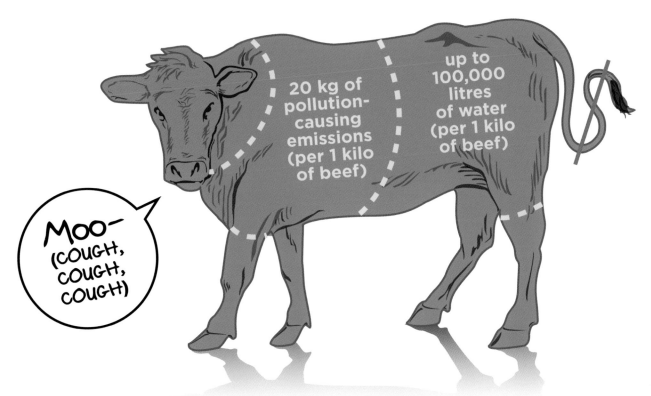

20 kg of pollution-causing emissions (per 1 kilo of beef)

up to 100,000 litres of water (per 1 kilo of beef)

Moo— (COUGH, COUGH, COUGH)

EARTH
Meat production creates 18% of man-made greenhouse gases.

SHRIMP
The average shrimp trawler emits 20 times more fuel than the small-fish industry.

PORK
One kilo of pork production releases over 7 kg of greenhouse gases.

LAND
1.4 hectares of land sustains a meat-eater. 0.2 hectares of land sustains a vegetarian.

GO TO PAGE 155 FOR MORE TIPS AND INFORMATION

Source: BBC's Bloom Project, *Scientific American*, Greenpeace and the International Development Research Centre (IDRC).

Knowledge is Power

Get Informed, Citizen

STOP THE PRESSES! We can't remember the last time we read a newspaper from cover to cover. Is that really a newsflash? Not really. The days when Dad used to spread out a copy of the newspaper and talk us through A1 to the classifieds, seem almost quaint today. We're busier than ever, multi-tasking while brushing our teeth or texting during work-outs. Only a fortunate few have time to flip through the newspaper.

But who says no news is good news? It's more important than ever to keep informed, stay engaged and stand up for the causes we believe in. We have to look to leaner, meaner and more efficient ways to get our need-to-know headlines, via podcasts, Facebook and Twitter, RSS Feeds and cell phone apps. Our personal favourite? We discovered a way to consume *The New York Times* before reaching the office each morning. We both subscribe to a read-aloud podcast of *The Times* from Audible.com. On any given morning, you can find either of us listening to an update on North Korea's missile program or a recent election in South America while searching for a missing sock or pouring milk on our Wheaties.

And we're not alone! The scales tipped in 2007 when online news gathered more readers than print. Today, less than 10 percent of North Americans rely on one media platform for information. Every day we meet busy, informed people who link up their on-the-go lives with a few clicks of a mouse or cell phone. They're media mavens or masters without the paper trail. And, when others tune out, they're showing up on election day in full force, voicing their well-informed opinions loud and clear.

GET ON THE INFORMATION SUPER HIGHWAY

- You've heard of the slow food movement, well now there's the slow reading movement. Turn off your Internet or phone and spend some solid time with a text.

- What good is a book sitting on your shelf? It may look nice, but that's not what books are for. Lend it to a friend and let those pages open up again.

- If you can't shoulder the cost of a newspaper subscription alone, share it with a roommate or family member.

- Most podcasts are free to download via iTunes. You can listen to the news on your walk to work or just use it to tune out annoying cell phone chatter on the commute.

- Try aggregators like Google News or an RSS feed to gather news sources from around the world.

- As Canadians, we like to be polite and steer clear of controversy in casual conversation. To heck with polite! Get in a meaningful discussion with someone today and share those opinions and views. You just might hear an interesting new take on a topic you overlooked before.

SOLID TIP

Q & A | *How do you stay current?*

EVAN SOLOMON, HOST OF CBC'S *POWER & POLITICS*

I read three or four daily papers and check news aggregating sites like NationalNewsWatch.com. Then there is the indispensable Twitter. I follow news organizations, key reporters, NGOs, leaders, MPs, and bloggers. This is the best place for breaking news, quick reactions and staying up-to-date. But, let me stress, staying current means having a deeper understanding and perspective through reading books, critical analysis and knowing a story's history.

CHARLOTTE EMPEY, EDITOR-IN-CHIEF ENGLISH NEWS, *METRO*

I read *Metro* and the other major papers every day for the big news of the day. I check the news stations on our office TVs and listen to radio news on my way to and from work for mainstream, need-to-know-right-now updates. And I turn to Twitter and Facebook to find out – yes, about offbeat events I'd never hear about otherwise. I'm insatiably curious about esoteric stuff – but primarily about the impact of news. What are people saying, thinking and feeling about the trending topics of the day or events in their communities? And I love Google Reader. It's an ideal way to catch up quickly on content from a range of different sources.

JORDAN BANKS, MANAGING DIRECTOR FACEBOOK CANADA, CONTRIBUTOR TO THE MARK, THEMARKNEWS.COM

No two days are ever the same for me so I've found that I'm highly reliant on my BlackBerry and my email system of sending myself links to read. One thing I do on Facebook is segment the people I've either friended or liked so that my wall is a more narrow filter that allows me to determine what it is I want to read or interact with, based on necessity. Sometimes it might be friends; sometimes it might be business publications. When you look at what happens on Facebook, what's often more interesting than the published article is the thread of commentary that happens below it. I actually learn more about public sentiment and trends and tones through the comments than I ever will through a static piece of journalism.

SAY WHAT?
IN ONE STUDY, 43% OF NORTH AMERICANS SAY IT WOULD DAMAGE CIVIC LIFE TO LOSE THEIR LOCAL NEWSPAPER, BUT 42% ALSO SAY THEY WOULDN'T MISS THEIR LOCAL PAPER IF IT SHUT DOWN.

GO TO PAGE 155 FOR MORE TIPS AND INFORMATION

It Shouldn't *Suck* to be You

Reduce Vampire Power

THERE'S A VAMPIRE STALKING YOUR HOME and we're not talking about those mournful, sparkly types from *Twilight*. This is something far more sinister: vampire power. That's the energy your appliances suck off the power grid without you even knowing about it. Think plasma TVs, laptops, cell phone chargers and the constantly ticking microwave clock – just for starters. It's a huge waste of energy!

Stats estimate that as much as 10 percent of home electricity is wasted through leaky sockets and appliances.   We know how much it stings when you lose money in your jacket. So, think about all the money and electricity you've wasted without your knowledge. You might have been a millionaire by now. Well, not really, but the problem is getting worse. Every year we buy more appliances, video game consoles and chargers; four billion cell phone chargers are sold every year. This means even more little plugs to siphon off our pennies. Don't think you can outsmart it by putting your Wii console on standby mode, and the same goes for appliances that are fully charged or turned off. Power is still trickling out as long as an appliance is plugged in, consuming anywhere from two to 20 watts of energy, which makes for one huge power suck. With something so simple to unplug, this is one beast that's easy to slay.

SOLID TIP

[YOUR NAME HERE] THE VAMPIRE POWER SLAYER

- Buy a power bar with an on-off switch to kill the power on multiple appliances with one switch.
- Dim the light on your TV and computer screen.
- Kill the quick-start button on your remote controls.
- Don't bother with stand-by mode; it still sucks power until you hit the switch.
- Consult www.cnet.com for tips on energy-efficient TV models.
- Look for Energy Star-rated appliances when you're in the market for a new electronic.

ENERGY VILLAINS

GAME CONSOLES

These entertainment systems suck away double and almost triple the amount of power than that of VCR and DVD players.

PLASMA TVS

These oh-so-fancy TVs suck two to three times more electricity than an average LCD screen TV.

CELL PHONE CHARGERS

Even when your cell is charged, it's still sucking power.

DESKTOP COMPUTERS

Laptops consume half the power of their massive desktop counterparts.

THAT HURTS...
A TYPICAL CANADIAN HOME USES 20 DIFFERENT PIECES OF EQUIPMENT THAT ALL CONSUME POWER IN STANDBY MODE.

GO TO PAGE 156 FOR MORE TIPS AND INFORMATION

Source: Efficiency NB, U.S. Department of Energy, *GOOD* magazine, Green Party of Canada and Cnet reviews.

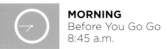

Telecommuting

To Leave or Not to Leave

ON THOSE MINUS 30 DEGREE Albertan winter days, Patricia Green is thankful she can work from home. The director of the Telus telecommuting program lives and often works from her house in St. Albert, a suburb of Edmonton. But then again, she could also be in Vancouver at a meeting or picking up her mail from her base office in Edmonton. In 2009, Telus rolled out the telework program to 18,000 staff members across Canada. Now, employees arrange schedules around life and work. For some, this could be as little as once a week in the office; others may follow a more traditional schedule. It saves energy (417, 216 kg of CO_2 in its first year!) and all those daily human costs of commuting. For Patricia, there's no more stressing about finishing work in time to make dinner for her two teenage boys. Now, returning to the 9-to-5 schedule would be the real grind.

This is the first generation in history that doesn't see showing up at the office as essential to our jobs. Everyone from Margaret Atwood to Alice Munro are using the aid of trusty devices, such as the so-called LongPen invention, to avoid climbing on yet another pollution-spewing airplane for a book tour. And today's online tools, such as Skype and Google, make this set-up accessible to everyone. One caveat though before you go phoning it in: telecommuting isn't a one-size-fits-all solution. Before you begin working in your pajamas, build a solid team base with face-to-face meetings, staff hang-outs and regular appearances at the office. This way you can have the best of both worlds: strong connections with your co-workers and a lighter carbon conscience.

SOLID TIP

THE NEW WORLD OF WORK

- Give your time management skills a work out in your home office.

- Make your house workspace distraction-free, clear of cell phones, pets and kids.

- Prepare lunches the night before, the same way you would going into the office, so you don't waste time prepping meals.

- Create time to meet informally with colleagues and build strong work relationships.

- When in the office, make the most of your presence by touching base with all team members.

- With an intense deadline looming, put a work-from-home arrangement on hold and assist your team.

THE WORK-FROM-HOME BALANCE

pros

- A worldwide survey found that 80% of teleworkers were as or more productive than their office counterparts.

- 33% of Canadians would take a work-from-home arrangement over a raise!

- Telework can be an option for those on maternity leave, a differently abled employee or one forced to relocate.

cons

- Working from home can increase feelings of isolation, while face-to-face interactions strengthen team member bonds.

- Studies show that non-teleworkers can feel a diminished sense of camaraderie with their telecommuting co-workers.

DID YOU KNOW...?
IF ONE MILLION CANADIANS WORKED FROM HOME JUST ONE DAY A YEAR, WE WOULD SAVE 250 MILLION KILOGRAMS OF CO_2 EMISSIONS AND 100 MILLION LITRES OF FUEL.

GO TO PAGE 156 FOR MORE TIPS AND INFORMATION

Source: Canadian Telework Foundation, the David Suzuki Foundation and Rensselaer's Lally School of Management and Technology study published 2008.

THE TELECOMMUTING WRITER
Margaret Atwood

The novels of Canada's most famous literary talent often paint a dire portrait of the planet years in the future and maimed beyond recognition. Margaret Atwood doesn't have it in for the environment. Her "speculative fiction" genre novels come out of a love for the environment and serve as a warning to change our ways. By reducing her own travels, carbon-offsetting when she can and using telecommuting tools, Margaret lives that lesson daily.

THE MOMENT: "He [my father] was a forest entomologist. They were avid gardeners all their lives, they had a city garden and a country garden. They grew a lot of vegetables. I remember in the Depression and the war, a lot of people grew a lot of vegetables."

THE MISSION: "I carbon offset. But there are mixed views about that. But again, the travel is actually quite small. If you carbon offset and also do extra insulation on your house, you're probably a bit ahead of the game."

THE HABIT: "If you take a small child, and I mean under two, out into nature, you will see instant interaction. They're much less bored when they're outside. And plastic gizmos are really no substitute unless you bring a child up entirely surrounded by plastic gizmos and they don't have any chance to turn on their epigenetic biophila switch. Just as if you bring a child up completely isolated from language, they won't be able to talk because it goes by developmental stages. So the biophilia switch is turned on early in life, or it's not. Maybe you have a mommy who says, 'Eww, dirty. Don't touch that. Come inside it's safer there.' Maybe you have that, and get really scared of being outside. But that's not a natural thing for people. It's much more natural for them to be comfortable outside."

MARGARET ATWOOD CHANGED
THE GAME FOR BOOK SIGNING
WITH HER LONGPEN

" *People talk about the environment as if it's something separate from them. But actually, you are a part of the environment.* "

Day

OFFICE POLITICS

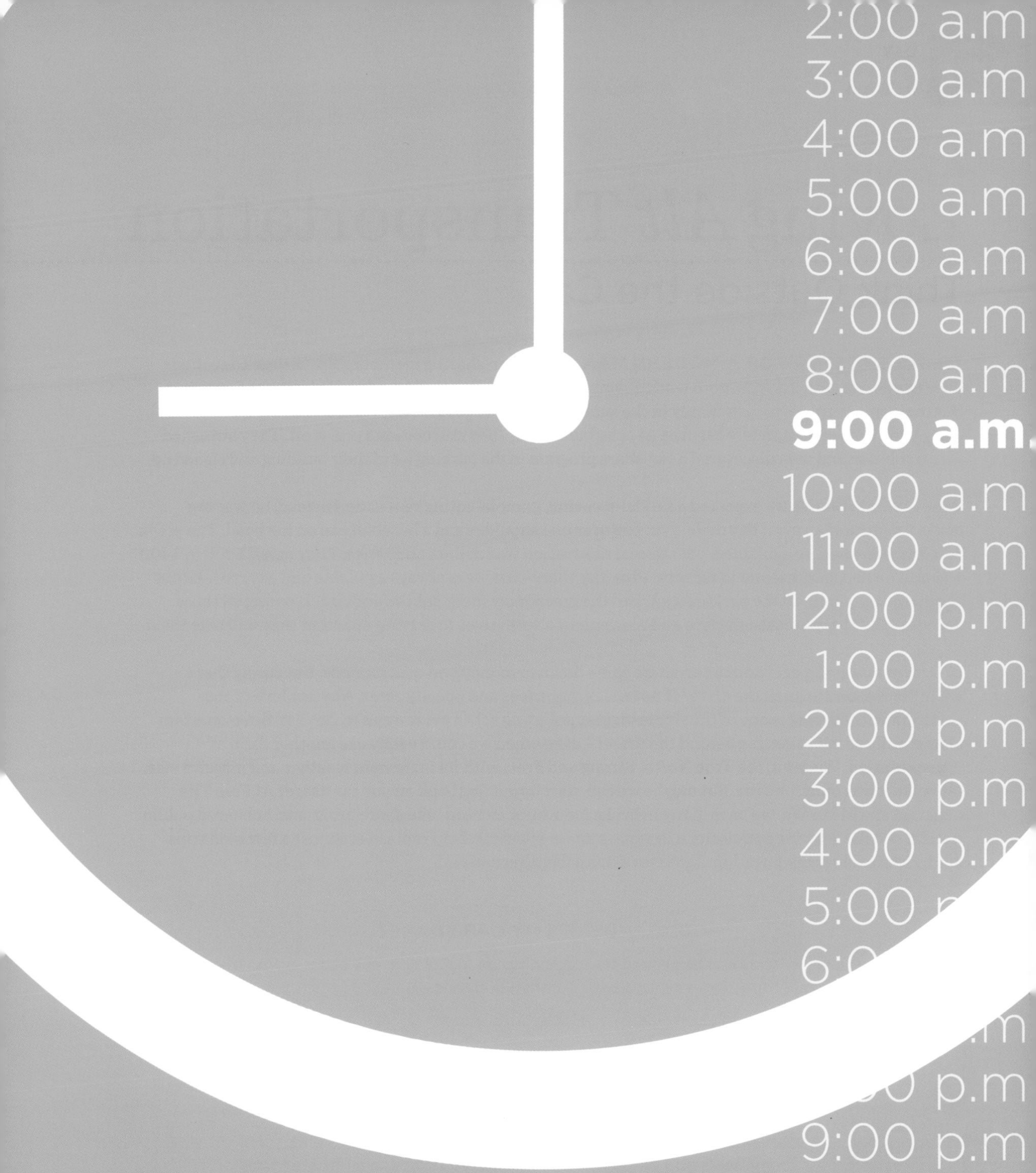

2:00 a.m
3:00 a.m
4:00 a.m
5:00 a.m
6:00 a.m
7:00 a.m
8:00 a.m
9:00 a.m.
10:00 a.m
11:00 a.m
12:00 p.m
1:00 p.m
2:00 p.m
3:00 p.m
4:00 p.m
5:00
6:
.m
0 p.m
9:00 p.m
10:00 p.m
11:00 p.m
12:00 a.m

Loving *Alt* Transportation

Think Outside the Car

THIS IS THE STORY OF A MODERN MAN and his car-sharing membership. George Dizvolitsis lives in a condo with his wife. Both work downtown, take public transit, and walk during the summer. But their epic journeys to visit family in the suburbs or trek to get groceries were wearing them down. They tried to be as completely car-free as possible and yet they still couldn't pull it off. They struggled with a solution and then discovered a car-share program in the parking lot of their building and signed up.

Before we met George we expected a sandal-wearing, granola-eating renegade. Instead, he was the perfect picture of an everyday dude, gym bag over one shoulder and a baseball cap on his head. The green benefits were nice, he explained, but the real motivation was dollars and sense. They saved $300 to $400 a month on fuel, parking and insurance. Plus, the share-cars were always available and easy to take out. We had an epiphany on the parking spot: had the green movement got the guilt pitch wrong all these decades? Give people cost-effective and convenient alternatives to driving a car and they will take them.

In George's case, the decision to car-share came down to money and convenience. But surely there are other reasons to ditch the drive? If not rising gas prices and obesity rates, why not love of the environment? Driving is one of the single biggest polluting acts a person can make. Yet, three quarters of us guiltily admit to getting behind the wheel – even when we could easily use another form of transportation. We get it, the True North, Strong and Free, with its inclement weather and massive size, feels like it was built for a car. But maybe we can start by cutting back on our car usage? At Free The Children and Me to We, we have many hybrids; for others, car and bike share programs, bolstered public transit, and the growing popularity of scooters and e-bikes can help replace even just a few road trips with sustainable transportation. Let's test drive a few alternatives!

DUDE, WHERE'S MY CAR SHARE?

- Try the walking school bus revolution, catching on in Ottawa and other cities, where children walk together in groups with parental supervision.

- Check out car-sharing companies available in your town or city.

- Bike-sharing options are popular at several universities across Canada, while the Bixi bike-sharing program is rolling in Toronto, Montreal and Vancouver.

- For the fast and fashionable, invest in an e-bike or scooter for quick, inter-city trips.

- Challenge yourself by leaving the car at home for a week. By week's end, you'll appreciate your wheels and pinpoint places where you can use alternate forms of transportation.

- Rural Canadians can scout out local bus and charter companies to get across back-country roads.

- When all else fails, plan ahead and carpool with neighbours or nearby families.

SOLID TIP

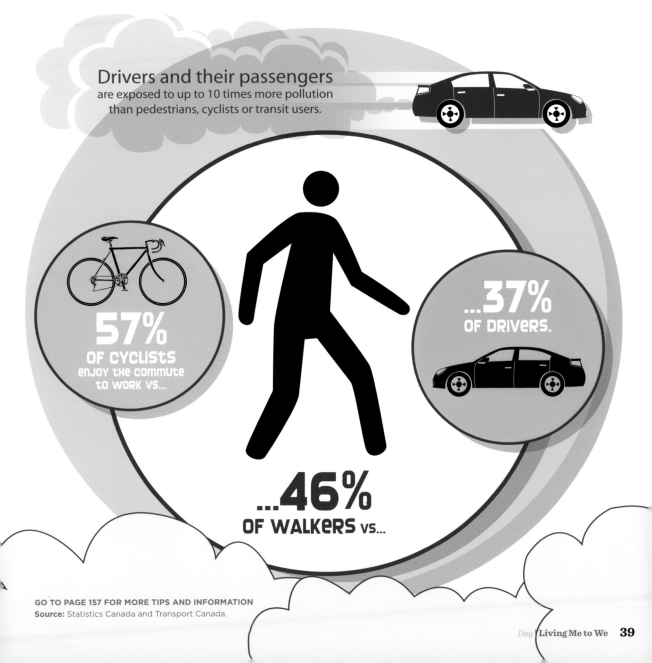

Drivers and their passengers
are exposed to up to 10 times more pollution than pedestrians, cyclists or transit users.

57%
OF CYCLISTS
enjoy the commute
to work vs...

...37%
OF DRIVERS.

...46%
OF WALKERS vs...

GO TO PAGE 157 FOR MORE TIPS AND INFORMATION
Source: Statistics Canada and Transport Canada.

Trips and *Trials*

Practice Commuter Etiquette

WELCOME TO YOUR MORNING COMMUTE. It's an early hour on a cold Canadian winter morning. The sun isn't even up yet. But there you are, waiting at a bus shelter as the snow and wind screech past. When the bus finally arrives, 20 people appear out of nowhere to rush the doors, while two exiting passengers battle their way off. Inside, you're affronted by blaring headphones, horrible personal odours – is that an onion bagel? – and a cell phone ringing unanswered somewhere in the bowels of the bus. Oh wait, it's just a passenger testing new ring tones. Then you hear a "clip-clip-clip" and realize someone is cutting his nails and you pray the stray slivers of personal matter don't land on you. The only available seat is claimed by a pair of wet UGG boots propped up by a sullen teenager. Getting off the bus has the feel of a prison break: pushing through textbook laden knapsacks and scrambling towards the exit before the bus lurches forward again. And this is a picture of a thoroughly big city commute. The spotty bus service in small town Canada – where a bus rumbles along the country road once every hour, if that – can make an urban transit user feel like he's won the lottery.

Canadians are a mild-mannered people, but occasionally poor commuter etiquette gets us biting our tongues and wishing for a saner world. Poster campaigns in Tokyo, New York and now Toronto condemn seat hoggers and litterers. Yet we all make exceptions for our own less-than-perfect behaviour when we've had a bad day or a rough sleep. So next time you feel your blood pressure rising on public transit because of hard-to-take hijinks or habits, ask yourself if the offense is serious enough to speak up. You can either chill – or challenge (gently). Someone genuinely might not know how loud her music is and informing her of that reality respectfully is not a criminal offence. You might even be doing a fellow comrade commuter a favour by speaking up. The best point of attack though is to pay someone a courtesy: make room unasked or help a mother with her stroller. These small acts can transform someone's grumpy morning mood and encourage others to pay it forward.

ROADSIDE OFFENCES

- Blaring headphones plus blaring cell phone chat equals blaring headache.
- No seat in site? Chances are it's worse for a pregnant, elderly or injured passenger.
- Paparazzi-style crowds that block the exits and entrances.
- I sit, therefore, I am. Your hockey bag doesn't merit that free seat.
- Drivers fond of resting elbows on car horns.
- Colour-blind bikers who coast through red lights.
- Cutting off, tailing and lane-hogging.
- Massive boxes or bikes taking up precious space during peak hours.
- Applying make-up in public is fine, but cutting toe-nails and plucking eyebrows?
- The public transit is not one big trashcan – save your throwaways for the bin.

TEMPERATURE RISING

What gets our blood boiling on the commute

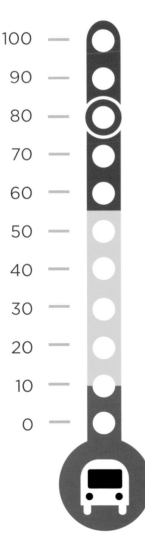

100
90
80
70
60
50
40
30
20
10
0

HOT

Loud Cell Phone Conversations

Blocking the Doors

Not Giving up a Seat to the Elderly or Pregnant

MEDIUM

Coughing without Covering Mouth

Stinky Take-out Food

Public Personal Upkeep

COLD

Reading over Shoulders

Stinky Breath, Bad Body Odour

GO TO PAGE 158 FOR MORE TIPS AND INFORMATION

*Electronic*Waste

Recycle That Old Cell Phone

WHERE ART THOU, FIRST-GEN SMARTPHONE? After the feeding frenzy over the new and shiny dies down, we rarely ask where old gadgets go. We met with Carole Hochu, Director of the Ontario Electronic Stewardship Program, to find out. Turns out your old phone, along with other electronic waste, could have been melted down and repurposed into Olympic medals at the Vancouver Winter Games as part of a unique recycling program. But few electronics have an awesome afterlife. Every year we produce 140,000 tonnes of electronic waste, much of it ending up on the trash heap, leaking toxins into the ground. Developing countries are burial sites for outdated gizmos where old computers and fax machines are picked apart by hand and rock, scavenged for parts and burned. These dumping grounds turn into toxic places, leading to high rates of cancer and lead poisoning for the people who live and work there.

With a bit of time and care, we can stop this epic fail. We've learned not to toss batteries out with our dinner; now it's electronics' turn. There are thousands of collection points across Canada to properly dispose of gadgets. (Penny pinchers take note: these recycling programs are funded by a levy included in the price of that electronic. You've already paid for the program, so you may as well make use of it, right?) Even better, donate your old, but still functional, computer, printer or office equipment to a charity or school. If you're the type who regularly upgrades your phone, pass that barely used cell on to less savvy friends and family. Whatever you do, don't toss those old electronics out with the trash.

REFRAIN AND REUSE

SOLID TIP

- Round up old electronics from the basement, attic and garage for one big massive recycle.

- Sometimes a new upgrade to a phone or a computer is just not that hot. Reading reviews of the latest toy and resisting to buy until a better release could save you money and time. (Check out: cnet.com or *Consumer Reports*)

- In the market for a new electronic something-something? Before you buy, check out Craigslist and other re-seller websites first. You may be able to find a perfectly good second-hand version.

- Check out Greenpeace's handy "Guide to Greener Electronics" before purchasing. It's a chance to support a company that makes a serious attempt at improving its environmental and social impact.

- Donate that old computer to the national Computers for Schools program, which refurbishes and then gives it to a school, library or learning centre in need.

SLIP SLIDING AWAY | *We love our phones ... and love to throw them away*

Less than 5% of cell phones are recycled.

14 million junked cell phones enter the garbage stream every 18 months.

Cell phones are replaced every 18 months.

GO TO PAGE 159 FOR MORE TIPS AND INFORMATION
Source: Canadian Wireless Telecommunication Association.

Me to We Workplace

Make Little Things Count

EVERY WEEK THE TEAM AT CLUB PENGUIN'S KELOWNA OFFICE breaks out a deck of cards and orders in pizza. On these once-a-week launch nights, the gang hangs out while uploading new videos and animation to Disney's entertainment site for kids. It's a tradition, even when the launch goes off without a hitch, to stay well into the night, playing cards and catching up. It's the unspoken rites around the office that make the Club Penguin team a tight one. Like the tea club (all dudes!) that initiates new hires by sampling a variety of brews or the weekly Thursday jams at a nearby co-worker's apartment. It's hard to tally every act, but the team at Club Penguin knows it's the little things that make a workplace truly special.

Common knowledge dictates that a happy worker is a more productive one, while studies show happiness can boost productivity by almost 15 percent! Sure, saying hello or asking about someone's weekend might feel like a struggle on Monday morning, but come Friday when the team needs to pull together on a project, the extra effort will pay off. These little extras cost nothing, but reap heaps of benefits in the department of mutual respect and teamwork. Cutbacks, downsizing, walk-outs and buy-outs: the new world of work can sometimes be a scary place. Never allow that malaise to set in, and we have a better chance at cheering one another on – and up.

LOOK OUT FOR EACH OTHER

- Upload your co-workers' birthdays into your calendar or smartphone. When the big day rolls around, send out an email with best wishes or stop by their desk to brighten their day.
- Take the extra time with someone's going-away card to remember personal moments that made a difference. Chances are this person helped you in some way. Now is the time to thank them.
- Have an upcoming event or rally you're excited to attend? Tell the whole office. Even if they're not keen on the issue, you'll discover new topics to talk about outside project updates.
- Keep a stack of blank gift cards in your desk for impromptu birthday or holiday celebrations.
- Office traditions make the workplace stronger. Bring back mementos from a trip to decorate the space or get the team to put together a mock newsletter of inside jokes.
- Create a team wall in a central space and post everyone's picture along with off-the-cuff descriptions of team members. This is an easy way to make newcomers feel they belong.
- Start a book or film club with team members outside the office.

SOLID TIP

CARING CULTURE

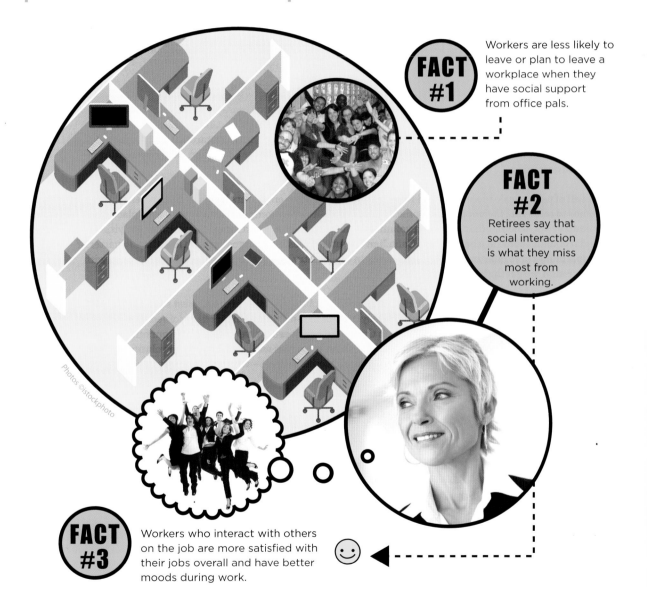

FACT #1

Workers are less likely to leave or plan to leave a workplace when they have social support from office pals.

FACT #2

Retirees say that social interaction is what they miss most from working.

FACT #3

Workers who interact with others on the job are more satisfied with their jobs overall and have better moods during work.

Photos ©istockphoto

GO TO PAGE 159 FOR MORE TIPS AND INFORMATION

Source: 2008 study published by Erasmus University Rotterdam, Tinbergen Institute and the CESifo Group.

DAY
Office Politics
10:05 a.m.

Corporate Social Responsibility 1.0

Volunteer with Your Colleagues

AT THE TOP OF MOUNT EVEREST François Langlois stood, surveying a view only a very few people have ever seen. Over the previous two years, he trained, sunk himself into debt (ironically enough for the Montreal financial advisor) and straggled along at the back of his climbing group up the mountain. Now that he had reached the top, he felt the urge to share the accomplishment with others. But how? A children's charity later approached François about raising money by leading climbs to some of the top peaks in the world. It was just the cause he'd been waiting for. Soon, he pitched his mission to his employer, Manulife Securities, which financed his flight to a climb in Antarctica and sponsored a fundraiser in Canada for the same charity. François has now raised over $4 million, doing something he loves to do.

Not all of us can scale mountains and raise millions, but today's employers have our back when it comes to achieving the impossible. Some 71 percent of Canadian companies encourage workplace volunteerism, whether that's creating volunteer time at work or supporting extracurricular activities. And it couldn't come at a better time: Canadian volunteer rates have stagnated with less than a quarter of people doing three quarters of the volunteering in the country. By combining professional pursuits with our passion, we get the best of both worlds.

In the winter of 2010, François reached his final goal: climbing all seven of the highest summits across seven continents. He didn't do it alone. A motley crew of like-minded climbers have joined him along the way. Introducing a social conscience into the workplace doesn't have to be a lonely pursuit for you, either. Ask around the water cooler or approach human resources with a plan to create volunteer days during or after work hours. Climb your own personal Mount Everest – who knows what's possible when you take your cause to the top.

TEAM EFFORT

SOLID TIP

- Suggest volunteer activities and meeting times that work around office hours, such as after work or during lunch.

- Get your boss involved! He or she may be able to help round up other interested employees or offer suggestions.

- Research an organization, then call up and ask how you or your team can partner on a volunteer project.

- Plan a group activity once a year as a group building experience.

- Host weekend activities and invite family and friends on board.

- Brainstorm specific skills you and your colleagues have to offer, such as accounting, lessons or a musical talent.

A NEW WAY TO WORK

*Couple your cause
with your workplace*

SURVEY SAYS

employees who volunteer are three times more likely to stay with their company.

CANADIANS

feel more connected to helping others directly, rather than cutting a cheque.

57%

of charitable organizations have difficulty finding the type of volunteers needed.

GO TO PAGE 160 FOR MORE TIPS AND INFORMATION
Source: Imagine Canada

Corporate Social Responsibility 2.0

Start a Responsible Work Culture

WELCOME TO 21ST CENTURY VOLUNTEERISM where business leaders have a unique opportunity to incorporate philanthropy into the office. From Telus donating mobile phones to emergency workers after Haiti's devastating earthquake to Walmart giving out energy-saving light bulbs to staff, there are so many ways for businesses to leverage their strengths. Look to domestic initiatives and figure out how to make volunteering a family activity for employees. It's easy for corporations to reinvent their image and create change using their products.

Travelling to new countries requires culture shock preparation. But Tania Carnegie could not have prepared for the KPMG employee trip to Kenya. Simply put: the people of the Maasai Mara rocked her world. Tania's been involved in community outreach for years but she met people in Africa who redefined what it meant to give back. They were working hard to make their small piece of the world a better place. Back in Canada, Tania and KPMG "adopted" three villages in the Maasai Mara, putting plans in place for sustainable water projects, alternative income, education and health care. But she felt the need to do more. Pretty soon, she drafted a plan to inspire KPMG employees to support their community year-round, just as she'd seen a world away in Kenya. Today the accounting company has one of the most ambitious corporate engagement programs in the country. Every employee – all 5,500 of them – is responsible for contributing to their community on his or her own terms, whether working in a community garden or building a home for low income families. Along the way, volunteers get help and support from Tania and the rest of KPMG's engagement staff.

SOLID TIP

TIPS FOR CEOS

- Pick a charity that is aligned with your brand to leverage for social good.

- Look to social media to get the word out about charitable initiatives.

- Start an annual awards ceremony, complete with staff nominations, to recognize the extra hours and hard work put in by employees.

- Create appreciation cards for employees to send to one another after a stellar project or volunteer effort.

- Encourage managers to become actively engaged in the company's volunteer projects and lead by example.

- Ask about payroll deduction programs with your human resources department, for quick, easy and regular donations to a charity of your choice.

- A volunteer trip is an excellent bonding exercise for a team. On your return, host an informal lunch time slideshow to share your initiatives and experiences with the rest of the staff.

STRONG COMPANY ROOTS | *A socially conscious company has room to grow*

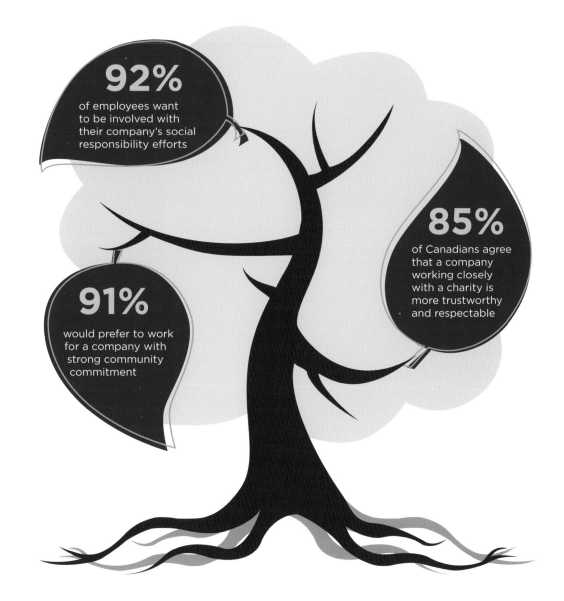

92% of employees want to be involved with their company's social responsibility efforts

85% of Canadians agree that a company working closely with a charity is more trustworthy and respectable

91% would prefer to work for a company with strong community commitment

GO TO PAGE 160 FOR MORE TIPS AND INFORMATION

Source: Imagine Canada, *Wall Street Journal.*

TRANSIT TOWN

Seamus O'Regan

When he's not getting up at the crack of dawn to host CTV's popular morning show *Canada AM*, Seamus O'Regan is out on the town riding streetcars, subways and buses. He's not doing it to make some grand point about saving the earth. He just genuinely thinks it's easier to ride transit. Okay, so maybe he has a bit of a crush on the environment.

THE MOMENT: "I grew up in Labrador, in a town of 8,000 people. If someone had lectured me back then that I shouldn't have a car, I would have laughed. How else was I supposed to get around? Back in those days, I had this real gas-guzzler: a big SUV. I loved that car. I had a bigger car than most people, but we all make mistakes and I would say that is mine. I've never forgotten how much money I spent on gas and how often I had to fill it up."

THE MISSION: "When I moved to Toronto, I decided I didn't need a car. In a city with way too many cars and too few roads, it just makes sense. I'm of the mind that you don't always have to make environmental choices because it feels good, but also because it makes sense. That's my kind of environmentalism."

THE HABIT: "Transit isn't perfect. As soon as I'm in a rush to go somewhere, I come out of my house and a bus goes by. It's like a quirk in *The Matrix*. But whenever I'm not in a rush, no problem, I make every connection. It's like, somehow, they know. During winter, it can get tough, but I'm pretty stubborn. I live at a corner where there's plenty of access to the streetcars, buses and subway. Instead of paying for parking everywhere and adding pollution to the air, taking transit just makes sense."

SEAMUS WAITING FOR THE
ICONIC TORONTO STREETCAR

66 *What's friendlier on the environment is often friendlier on the pocket book, too."*

Day

MONEY
MATTERS

2:00 a.m.
3:00 a.m.
4:00 a.m.
5:00 a.m.
6:00 a.m.
7:00 a.m.
8:00 a.m.
9:00 a.m.
10:00 a.m.
11:00 a.m.
12:00 p.m.
1:00 p.m.
2:00 p.m.
3:00 p.m.
4:00 p.m.
5:00 p.m.
6:0
.m.
00 p.m.
9:00 p.m.
10:00 p.m.
11:00 p.m.
12:00 a.m.

Put Your Money Where Your *Heart* Is

Invest for Change

ONCE A CITY PLANNER FOR THE CITY OF VICTORIA, Dennis Carlsen now consults on green and affordable housing projects in Vancouver. He thought he was pretty up-to-date on environmental and social issues – until he took a closer look at his RRSP. Why was a tobacco company in his portfolio when his father died of lung cancer? But his advisor was more interested in rates of returns than feel-good finances. So Dennis made a move – to an ethical investor. Today Dennis' portfolio is stuffed with SRIs (socially responsible investments) such as housing trusts and green technology. If Dennis wants more information on a company's background, his advisor outlines its past. If he questions a certain holding, his advisor explains how ethical shareholders and investors leverage holdings to get a company to improve its record. Together they're figuring out a better roadmap for how to invest.

Could it be that the Gordon Gekko era of "greed is good" is fading? Today, ethical investing is a $609 billion industry in Canada. Socially responsible companies are increasingly seen as better value for money over the bad boys of the investing world. The logic runs like this: companies that treat workers well or upgrade environmentally will avoid major costs when government regulations and other restrictions kick in later. Today, traditional holdings earn nearly the same as ethical stocks. For every early adopter like Dennis, who would choose the common good over profits regardless, ethical investment options continue to expand. We can increasingly make a buck and do good at the same time. Speak to your advisor about SRIs or turn to the Social Investment Organization's cross-Canada listings for advice. Get informed and don't be afraid to ask the tough questions.

SOLID TIP

THE STEPS TO SOCIALLY RESPONSIBLE STOCK

- Each industry has its own environmental or social issues to wade through. Ask your advisor which companies are leaders or laggards when it comes to instituting changes.

- Raise the topic of corporate social responsibility with your advisor. It's his or her job to know.

- You can't just walk into any old bank branch and talk investments. All major banks have a special investment branch. Make an appointment there.

MY WAY OR THE HIGHWAY

Figure out whether your advisor can help you in your pursuit of socially responsible stock

THE MAKE-NO-MONEY ARGUMENT Your investor may say that SRIs make no green.

COUNTERARGUMENT The pay-off may not be as speedy as a literal goldmine, but you can have peace of mind that you're investing in stock that is responsible. Plus, you're supporting a growing number of SRIs that will hopefully become the norm.

THE "MO'TIME, MO'MONEY" LOGIC Your advisor may say ethical investments require more research and time and, therefore, higher management fees.

COUNTERARGUMENT If your advisor can't accommodate your values without an extra charge, take your money elsewhere.

THE "HIGHER-FEES" PROPOSITION An advisor might say that SRI mutual funds cost more in fees.

COUNTERARGUMENT Management fees of ethical mutual funds are typically on par with conventional ones. This is a mostly unfounded myth.

TIME TO FIND A NEW ADVISOR Got a lame duck advisor? The Social Investment Organization can help you out with its Canada-wide listing of advisors.

DO YOUR HOMEWORK: KNOW THESE TERMS

ESG: Environmental Social Governance
Your advisor may refer to ESG, which stands for Environmental Social Governance factors and look at the long term of investment.

"Best in Class"
Also called "industry agnostic," the "best in class" approach singles out and excludes the least responsible players within a certain industry.

GO TO PAGE 161 FOR MORE TIPS AND INFORMATION
Source: Jantzi-Sustainalytcis.

Paperless Finances

Get Your Bank On

THE TRIP TO THE BANK MACHINE is rarely fun, especially when it spits out a piece of paper confirming your ever-shrinking account balance. But stop to consider the paper evidence of that transaction. Many of us choose to print a receipt almost unconsciously, but that adds up to an estimated 16.5 million trees every year. That's a whole lot of lumber just to hear you're broke. Again.

But believe it or not, bank receipts are one of the top sources of litter in the world and Canadian forests are paying the price. Along with Russia, Canada has the most forests in the world and the worst track record for clear cutting them: 90 percent of our logging comes from old-growth Boreal trees that take 200 years to regenerate. Every year, a swath of forest larger than Prince Edward Island disappears from Alberta, British Columbia and Ontario. And yet, that recycled icon that pops up on books or tissue dupes us into thinking the paper abundance comes from sustainable or recycled sources. That's the exception, not the rule.

Paper hounds our every move, whether we want it to or not. Tell the cashier you don't want a receipt – too late, it's already printed. Remember to say you don't need cutlery with a take-out order, then find a wad of napkins stuffed in the, gulp, paper bag. Instead, call the shots when you can. Skip the paper receipt at the bank machine or display the balance on screen (not recommended at dodgy street corners late at night, of course). Lose the paper trail with all your financial activities. Electronic tax filing is greener and more accurate anyway. With banks beefing up online security and often reimbursing customers for any losses through fraud, it's safer than ever to choose Internet banking. With mobile banking catching on to a smartphone near you, the bank machine will soon be out of the picture entirely! Unfortunately, that depressing bank balance might stay the same.

CLEAR-CUT ALTERNATIVES

FSC

- Look for the Forest Stewardship Council (or FSC) mark on all the paper you purchase. This is the most trusted mark of good forest management in the world.

- Ask your boss to switch to recycled paper at work.

- Think before you print. If you do hit print, use both sides of the page.

- Switch to automatic deposit for your paycheque.

- Purchase tax-filing software and do your taxes electronically.

- Sign up for paperless credit card, bank statements – and even avoid the mailed bills for magazine subscriptions or gym memberships.

- Do away with paper cheques by signing up for email money transfer technology.

- Keep a collection of reusable paper around the house.

SOLID TIP

SKIPPING THE PAPER

SAY NO TO RECEIPTS

Opt out of printing a receipt, and North Americans could save a roll of paper 609,600 metres long – enough to circle the earth fifteen times.

AUTOMATIC DEPOSITS

Switching to automatic deposits for paycheques could save $65 billion in fuel and lost time costs.

DID YOU KNOW?

North Americans use approximately 37 billion cheques a year.

GO TO PAGE 161 FOR MORE TIPS AND INFORMATION
Source: *The Green Book.*

DAY
Money Matters
12:30 p.m.

Anyone can
be a Philanthropist

Stretch Your Pennies

THESE DAYS THE WORD "PHILANTHROPIST" is often associated with a Bill Gates billionaire-type bequeathing a mega fortune on multiple charitable causes. But in the dictionary the word still keeps its humble meaning: someone with a love for humanity. At Free The Children we meet philanthropists every day; oftentimes it's a 12-year-old cradling a jar of hard-won pennies. Soon after, an all-call email gets sent out: "Hey team, who wants to roll pennies this lunch break?" In the non-profit world where a dollar can mean the difference between a child learning in a classroom or working in a field, every penny counts and must be counted! It's time for us to take back the word "philanthropist." With the help of a few tried-and-true tips to stretch those pennies further, we can all turn chump change into *real* change.

It's not always easy, of course, to be a savvy philanthropist. As headlines trumpet the next major disaster or highlight the latest charity scandal, it's easy to fall into donor fatigue. Then we run the risk of shutting ourselves off from the real need out there. Following a few general rules can help. Before you donate, ask yourself whether an organization is offering systemic change or just a short-term solution. For instance, is it helping the roots of hunger or just filling bellies temporarily? Next, remember that just because you've heard a charity's name doesn't make it a reliable choice. Charities often get their name out there through advertising or canvassing campaigns that cost thousands or millions of dollars of money that could be helping a real cause. Finally, look for high-touch organizations that make it easy to talk with a real person about where your money is going and who the dollars are helping. There are many ways to ensure your money gets where you want it to go.

SOLID TIP

MAKE YOUR DOLLAR GO THE DISTANCE

- Make sure the charity is registered with the Canada Revenue Agency (look for its charity number).

- A registered charity is not required to provide a donor with an official tax receipt so after providing your name and address, request one and save it for your records.

- Tax credit rates on charitable donations vary widely between provinces and territories, from Quebec's 35 percent down to Nunavut's 19 percent, combining both provincial and federal credits.

- Raise your donation to over $200 and your tax credit will get a substantial boost across Canada, although the percentage depends on the province.

- Thinking of making a will or bequest to benefit a cause? Get a lawyer to fill out the forms properly for you, make sure you check the charity's registration number and include specific directions on how the money can be spent.

- Attach a note to your donation, specifying exactly who or what the money should help and how. A Canadian charity is under strict obligations to follow that request.

- Read the organization's annual report, which should be clearly linked on its homepage. This helps clarify how every dollar is spent.

ASK BEFORE YOU DONATE

Check out Imagine Canada, the voice of Canadian charities, for their Ethical Code Handbook and more information.

GO TO PAGE 162 FOR MORE TIPS AND INFORMATION
Source: Imagine Canada, Free The Children.

Creative *Donations*

Give the Big and Small

NOTEBOOKS AND PENCIL SHARPENERS, coloured construction paper, tennis balls, soap, bandages and (unused) toothbrushes: this is just the tip of the iceberg when it comes to off-the-wall donations we receive at Free The Children. In the non-profit world, the big-hearted are not necessarily the big-walleted. Arts supplies are packed up into school kits and shipped overseas. Medical supplies are delivered to impoverished hospitals. Kids, adults and corporations all donate in different ways, putting to good use what they have. A corporation might donate a personal accounting session for non-profit workers or offer up old, but still usable, office equipment. Once a child outgrows her training wheels, she can donate her old bike to a child without one. You might choose to give away those old glasses taking up space in your drawer or the sneakers kicking around your closet.

But keep this golden rule in mind: if you wouldn't use that rusty old washing machine, then don't give it away. Some things truly are meant for the trash. For instance, does anyone actually buy second-hand underwear at Goodwill? Donating goods past their prime can even cut into a charity's cash flow, doing more harm than good. The Salvation Army, for instance, was forced to shell out $30,000 to dispose of dumped garbage and wrecked donations in Woodstock, Ontario. Next time you want to donate, get on the phone with your charity of choice and ask specifically what non-monetary donations they need. Who knows what garden, garage or home office odds and ends they could be after?

SOLID TIP

ONE MAN'S TRASH...

- Ask a local school music department or a daycare if they accept instruments.
- If an organization can't directly use or take a donation, sell the object at a garage sale, junk shop or online and donate the proceeds.
- Unused renovation materials, such as paint, windows, doors, lumber and lighting fixtures, can be donated to Habitat for Humanity's ReStores as well as other organizations.
- Look into getting the cash value of your donation assessed by a third-party.
- Even if the hunk of junk is broken down in the driveway, you can still donate it to a charity or someone in need through programs such as CharityCars, CarHeaven and others.
- Old electronics (computers, printers and the like) are often in high demand by cash-strapped charities.
- Ask if the charity will pick up the equipment for you.
- Animal shelters accept unopened wet and dry food as well as toys, pillows, leashes and other pet accessories. Make sure to check with your local shelter before dropping off your contribution.

THE LIFE OF A PIANO

STEP ONE

An elderly couple was moving to a retirement home and looking to donate their old piano to charity.

TAX RECEIPT

STEP TWO

Free The Children used a certified appraiser to determine the value of the piano and procured a charitable donation receipt for the couple.

STEP THREE

The piano is now in one of Free The Children's Kenyan schools and continues to make music.

GO TO PAGE 162 FOR MORE TIPS AND INFORMATION
Source: Free The Children.

LOW-IMPACT BAND

Barenaked Ladies

With songs about pining for a million dollars to splurge on tree houses and K-cars, the Barenaked Ladies have endeared themselves to millions of Canadians as down-to-earth dudes. Literally. The Ladies take their impact on the earth very seriously when they tour, always seeking out ways to recycle, reduce and reuse.

THE MOMENT: "There are so many artists who really believe in being environmentally and socially responsible in their daily lives. Actually, many even work it into their lyrics. Then you go on tour and wonder how much of an impact you can really have. That's what happened to us. All day, we're driving in big buses, burning fuel all over the place, playing in these arenas with disposable everything and huge amounts of wattage being used just by the lights."

THE MISSION: "We partnered with a group called Reverb, started by a friend of ours, Adam Gardiner from the band Guster. They were essentially a bunch of socially and environmentally conscious artists working in an industry that had no conscience at all. Together, we look at ways to change how we do business: burning alternative fuels like bio-diesel on buses, using real cutlery backstage and LED lights that use 80 per cent less energy."

THE HABIT: "It's sometimes hard touring in remote areas where it's hard to get the right fuel or there's no recycling facility. We've hauled these things around until we've found a depot. We also recruit fans through our Barenaked Ladies Planet Initiative. Fans come back and have a meet-and-greet with the band if they pledge to look after the recycling after the gig. It's about getting our fan base involved and taking initiative in our business to make a difference. Traditionally there's a lot of waste, but more and more artists are realizing how easy it is to change the way you do things."

THE BAND ON THE ROAD

" *Every problem looks insurmountable until you take action.*"

Day
COMMUNI
TIES

2:00 a.m.
3:00 a.m.
4:00 a.m.
5:00 a.m.
6:00 a.m.
7:00 a.m.
8:00 a.m.
9:00 a.m.
10:00 a.m.
11:00a.m.
12:00 p.m.
1:00 p.m.
2:00 p.m.
3:00 p.m.
4:00 p.m
5:00
9:00 p.m.
10:00 p.m.
11:00 p.m.
12:00 a.m.
TY

The *Power* of *Walking*

Create a Community Connection

IMAGINE THE STREET your mother told you never to walk down at night: dripping pipes, shadowy corners and exhaust vents spewing fog. During a midnight tour of Vancouver's notorious east side, we walked that street. Known as a SLAP tour, this walk explores the forgotten underside of Canada's poorest neighbourhood where we met addicts, drug dealers and street workers. One teen said it was his first night sleeping outside after getting kicked out of a Tim Hortons. We realized how little we knew the city we had visited countless times before; we were always rushing past with blinders on. It took a walk to slow us down and rediscover the many stories of the street.

No one enjoyed a good walk or appreciated its illuminating power more than urban thinker and writer Jane Jacobs. Refering to of the "intricate sidewalk ballet" of the streets, she invited all of us to step outside our bubbles and see how we fit into the larger world. Speeding past in a car, you miss the details of the changing streetscape: the shutters of a fourth-generation store, the young family carrying a new baby or the kid sleeping in a doorway. Meanwhile, postal carriers, who walk the same blocks daily, are so in sync with the community they are often first to report crimes or help at the scene of an accident. Most importantly, a walkable community is an accessible community. For the elderly lady who recently lost her license or the poor student who can't afford a car, the sidewalk is the ultimate leveller and a space we can all learn to share.

What's good for your community also works wonders for your health and the environment. Walking one kilometre a day reduces your risk of obesity by 5 percent. Plus, it produces no pollution and costs nothing, except maybe a new pair of walking shoes now and again. Whether you walk to raise money for cancer, learn about an issue like homelessness or simply to get from point A to B, take the time to slow down the fast pace of your world and reconnect.

WALK THIS WAY

- Take or lead a Jane's Walk, a walking festival that happens every May across Canada.
- Start a morning or evening walking group in your neighbourhood. Committing to a group plan means you're much more likely to make the trek.
- Pick an area of your town or city you've never explored and spend the weekend there on foot.
- When moving to a new neighbourhood, rank it based on whether you can reach the nearest school, library, grocery store, park and hardware store on foot. Or enter the postal code on Walkscore.com, which will instantly assess the 'hood's walkability.
- Dogs are a great way to work in a daily walk, not to mention the companionship of an animal friend.
- Try to walk one errand a day.

SOLID TIP

····| GRADE YOUR 'HOOD | *Look for these signs that you live in a walkable area.*

BUSINESSES AND SCHOOLS: Are there nearby spots to work and learn?

SCHOOL

PUBLIC SPACE: Are there public parks or green areas?

PEOPLE: Are the streets buzzing with people?

GROCERY STORES AND ENTERTAINMENT: Can you grab essentials nearby? Can you walk to a local pub, movie theatre or café?

"My feet are my only carriage, so I've got to push on through."
BOB MARLEY

GO TO PAGE 163 FOR MORE TIPS AND INFORMATION
Source: Jane's Walk, Walkscore.

Take the *Lead*

Become a Mentor

AS CRAIG WAITED BACKSTAGE at a fundraiser for the Big Brothers Big Sisters of Canada, he saw a middle-aged man helping an elderly gent to his seat. Father and son, Craig assumed, until an organizer standing beside him whispered: "That's why we do what we do." The organizer explained further: Little Brother, now in his 50s, was returning the help and guidance of his now elderly Big Brother 30 years later. Craig went onstage to give his speech all choked up. It perfectly demonstrated the lasting power of mentorship.

Mentoring has existed in some form for centuries. Trades relied on apprentices to pass on skills and tribal elders prepared their youth for vision quests. Though the world is as much in need of mentors as ever, today mentorship is often missing in action. Today kids wait upwards of two years to get a mentor through specialized programs. Teachers barely have time to cover the curriculum, let alone take on mentorship roles. Yet studies show that kids are struggling in a vacuum: with a mentor in their lives they are 80 percent more likely to finish high school and 46 percent more likely to steer clear of illegal drugs.

The beauty of mentorship is that anyone can do it. New Canadians are often paired up with someone from their own ethnic community to help explain cultural differences or to find a job. University and college grads can offer invaluable tips to students nervous about entering the workforce. Forward-thinking businesses and organizations often pair up new employees with veterans – think *The Apprentice* without the cameras or Donald Trump's hair. If 30 years from now your mentee is still by your side, helping you into a chair, you'll know you made an impact on someone's life.

HELP THE LITTLE GUY

- Keep your eyes and ears open for mentoring possibilities through your network of friends and family. Ask to be introduced to someone with valuable expertise or offer your time to a newbie in your field.

- Contact school guidance offices or community centres for available mentoring opportunities. Think of Scouts, Big Brothers Big Sisters, Boys and Girls Club, YMCA and other local groups.

- Have a niche interest or passion – say, boat building or book collecting? Offer to do a presentation at a nearby school or library.

- Sign up with your human resources department at work as a mentor to new hires. For the new hires out there, ask for a mentoring partnership from more senior employees.

- Many universities and colleges have mentorship programs through which you can make valuable contacts and life-long friendships.

- Starting a new business? Entrepreneurial mentorships are common and fruitful partnerships in the business world. Call up a business person you admire, introduce yourself and your project, and suggest coffee or lunch on you.

SOLID TIP

MAKE IT MATTER | *Children who have a mentor figure in their lives are:*

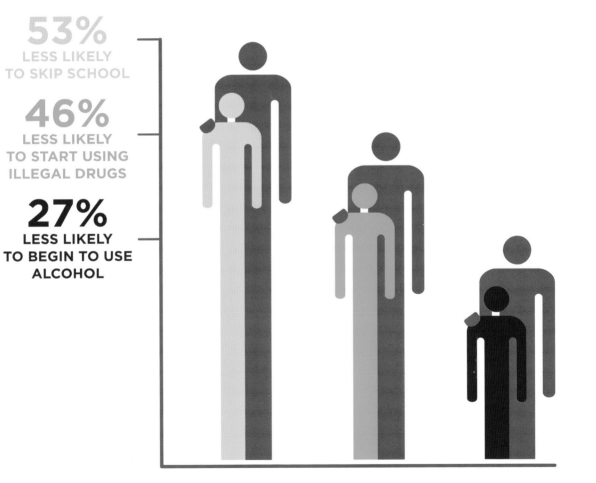

53%
LESS LIKELY
TO SKIP SCHOOL

46%
LESS LIKELY
TO START USING
ILLEGAL DRUGS

27%
LESS LIKELY
TO BEGIN TO USE
ALCOHOL

GO TO PAGE 164 FOR MORE TIPS AND INFORMATION

Source: Government of British Columbia, British Columbia Crime Prevention Association.

Beyond the Ballot Box

Get Politically Involved

LONG BEFORE CHILD SLAVERY stirred Craig to action, he honed his change-making chops with community issues. After he discovered his local library was slated to close, he hopped on his bike and headed to a public meeting on the closure. Craig was nervous, even with a group of pals at his side for moral support. Taking a deep breath, he delivered his appeal to the crowd: "This is where we go after school until our parents get home. If the library closes, maybe we'll just go sit in front of the TV. Aren't adults always telling us not to do this?" Craig was surprised to hear applause fill the room. He was even more surprised when library advocates later asked him to address city council. At the age of 11, years before he could cast a vote or become a politician, Craig realized he had the power to weigh in and affect real-world decisions.

Every few years we're called to that cardboard station to tick a box and afterward we walk out feeling, well, less than civically engaged. Voting, although supremely important to democracy, is a pretty banal act. So, instead of voting once every two or three years, how about we turn every day into election day, every letter to the editor into our own personal soapbox, every social media post into a lively debate? By taking it upon yoursel to become informed and involved in an issue, you make the cause part of your life. Look for candidates who care about your issue, from the municipal up to the federal level, and help out on his or her campaign now, not just right before an election. Make your voice heard at council meetings and rallies. Make your presence felt at marches and fundraisers. Each act and each day is a way of voting for a better world.

WAYS TO ENGAGE

- Get acquainted with local groups doing work that you want to get involved in.
- Write a petition or a letter to the editor.
- Follow your local MP on Twitter or Facebook and don't be afraid to send remarks of your approval or disapproval of their work.
- Donate to a political party or join one.
- Ask to meet with your city councillor, MP or MPP.
- Politicians often say that one letter or email counts as the views of 100 people. What better reason to pick up a pen or fire off an email?
- Put a sign on your lawn, website or Facebook page.
- Volunteer at a campaign headquarters for a candidate of choice.
- Invite an inspiring candidate into your community group to speak.
- Pick your candidate well in advance of the election and start supporting him or her now.

SOLID TIP

CAST YOUR VOTE

It's time we all stepped up to the ballot box.

CLOSE TO 40% OF VOTERS DIDN'T BOTHER TO TURN UP IN THE 2011 ELECTION.

HALF A MILLION YOUTH UNDER VOTING AGE PARTICIPATED IN THE MOCK STUDENT VOTE INITIATIVE.

GO PEI! THE ISLANDERS HAVE HAD THE BEST TURN-OUT RATE IN THE LAST FIVE ELECTIONS FROM 2000 TO 2011.

GO TO PAGE 164 FOR MORE TIPS AND INFORMATION
Source: Statistics Canada, Student Vote, *National Post*.

The Greatest *Gift*

Share Your Health

ANGELISA LAKE SERVES classic Maritime fare at a Charlottetown pub, but in her off hours, she's an everyday superhero. The 23 year old has faithfully donated blood for years. One day, she picked up a brochure on OneMatch, Canada's stem cell and bone marrow registry. With a quick swab of the mouth, sent off in the mail, Angelisa was in the system. Time passed and, despite the odds, a patient match was found. Later, as she donated her stem cells in a Halifax hospital and cancer patients shuffled past her in the ward, she was reminded again of how important her donation was. (Currently, less than one percent of Canada's population is on the registry.) A few hours waiting in a hospital on Angelisa's part could literally save someone's life.

Canada, a country so rich in health services, is near impoverished when it comes to sharing our health with each other. Less than 4 percent of us donate blood, but 52 percent say they or a family member have needed blood. If you can't donate the red stuff, Canada's stem cell and bone marrow registry needs help, too. Many confuse stem-cell donation with embryonic stem cells, but they're actually an immature part of our blood that can morph into any other cell in our blood stream. Our diversity – something we normally consider Canada's greatest attribute – is a serious obstacle when it comes to stem cells. Caucasians currently make up 82 percent of donors, but matches are made along ethnic lines meaning minority groups may struggle to find a donor. There are other ways to get creative with sharing your health. Clinics accept donated breast milk , cancer organizations need hair for wigs, while a pregnant woman can donate her stem cell-rich umbilical cord after giving birth. As Angelisa can attest, donating your health is a powerful gift that costs nothing but a little time.

BLOOD BUDDIES

SOLID TIP

- Signing up to OneMatch's stem cell and bone marrow registry is easier than ever, done both online and through the mail. Go to OneMatch.ca, fill out the form and the test is sent via post.

- Check out OneSight and other organizations that accept donations of old eyeglasses that can be passed on to the one billion people around the world who need glasses.

- Donate old medical supplies – wheelchairs, walkers, crutches, unused incontinence pads, diapers, bath towels – to organizations like the StarFish Project that ship supplies to HIV clinics in Nigeria.

- Grow your hair for someone else! Donate your long hair to programs like Cuts for Cancer that create wigs for cancer patients.

- Make sure to fill out your organ donation cards and inform your family of your wishes. Many provinces include the organ donation card when you receive a driver's license.

- Keep up-to-date on the changing rules and regulations around donating blood.

SNAPSHOT OF CANADIAN BLOOD

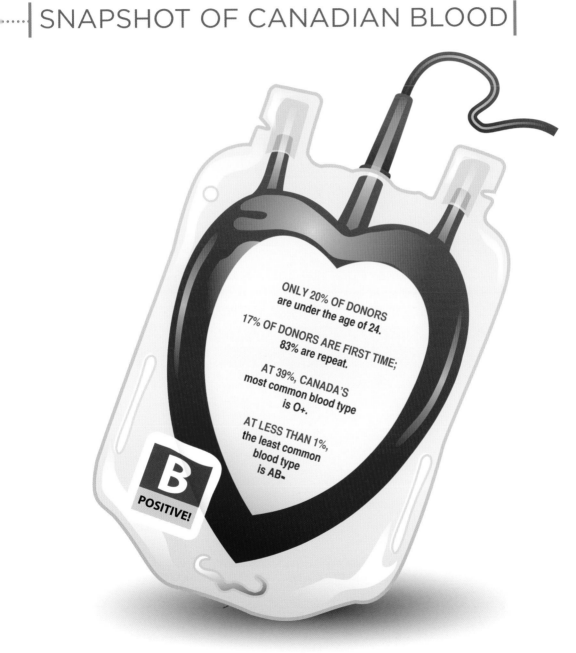

ONLY 20% OF DONORS are under the age of 24.

17% OF DONORS ARE FIRST TIME; 83% are repeat.

AT 39%, CANADA'S most common blood type is O+.

AT LESS THAN 1%, the least common blood type is AB-.

B
POSITIVE!

GO TO PAGE 166 FOR MORE TIPS AND INFORMATION
Source: Canadian Blood Services.

Skill *Swap*
Give What You're Good At

AT HIS CHIC SALON in Ottawa, Marwan El Rassi trims the locks of not only the rich and powerful (Jean Chrétien and Paul Martin have been his clients), but also the downtrodden and disadvantaged. Growing up in Lebanon, Marwan had a deep appreciation for women instilled in him by his strong mother. When he left for Canada and opened his own salon, he wanted to give back to disadvantaged women neglected by society. So, twice a year he closes shop and invites women from the local women's shelter, Maison D'Amitié, for an afternoon of haircuts, dye jobs and highlights – all *gratuit*. Decorating the salon with fresh flowers and setting out goodies – all donated from nearby businesses – on china plates, he and his staff pamper the women who have lived on the street or escaped abusive relationships. At day's end, the women leave with a fresh cut of confidence.

The hair we cut, the taxes we account for and the buildings we design – these are the skills that earn our daily bread and they're more valuable than money in the bank. The skills we donate have real monetary value: just look at the $14 billion dollars worth of volunteer hours Canadians donate every year (the equivalent of 1.4 percent of Canada's GDP!). Of course, we understand that when many people punch out at the end of the day they like to leave that work right where they left it – at work! But isn't it refreshing to think that the world of volunteering is not just stuffing envelopes or answering phones? Teaching, mentoring, bookkeeping and counselling have all become top volunteer activities. Plus, creating an informal volunteer opportunity is the easiest way to identify a real need in your area. Your work could reach one person, such as through tutoring a youngster in math, or a group, like a grassroots organization in need of consulting advice. Helping in this personal way means you'll get to see the fruits of your labour up close.

DO WHAT YOU LOVE

SOLID TIP

- Brainstorm your skills, both professional and amateur, as well as all the people, events and organizations that might benefit from them.

- Think of skills outside your typical workday, such as reading or listening, which can easily be donated to hospital patients or the elderly in need of companionship.

- Check out websites (such as Getinvolved.ca) that pair skilled people with organizations in need where you can post your skill or search a certain kind of organization.

- Stay engaged with the organizations you want to help, keeping track of upcoming drives and events.

- Play an instrument? Have a golden voice? Donate your chops to an old folks' home or community centre talent night – who knows, you might just garner some new fans!

WANTED: VOLUNTEERS!

Some 57% of charitable organizations struggle to find volunteers with skills they need. Volunteers do a range of duties – not just stuffing envelopes – and of those surveyed:

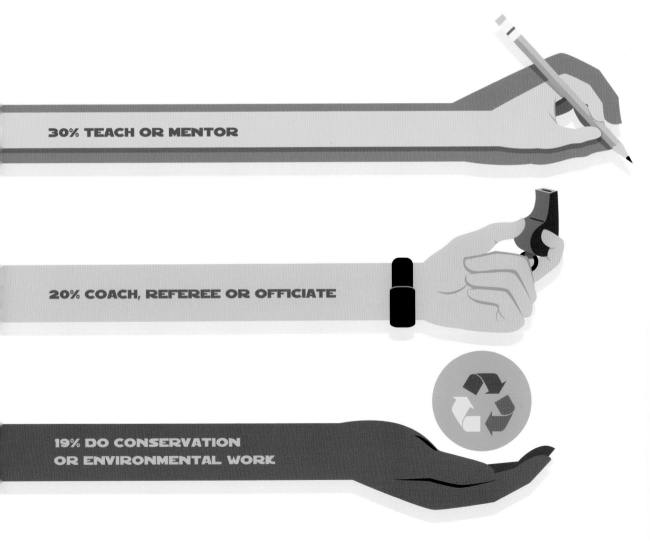

30% TEACH OR MENTOR

20% COACH, REFEREE OR OFFICIATE

19% DO CONSERVATION OR ENVIRONMENTAL WORK

GO TO PAGE 166 FOR MORE TIPS AND INFORMATION

Source: Imagine Canada.

Raise Your *Voice*

Get Engaged Through Social Media

SPRINKLED AMONGST TACO RECIPES and family outing ideas, Andrea Tompkins's blog A Peek inside the Fishbowl tackles thorny community issues in her Westboro neighbourhood in Ottawa. Back in 1999, Andrea began documenting her daily life as a young mother online. But, in 2007, the blog became her soapbox as well. A 1930s convent near her home was slated for removal to make way for monster homes that she feared would destroy the heritage and harmony of her 'hood. So Andrea took to her blog, posting updates on council meetings, breaking news and impassioned pleas to city councillors and locals to save the building. Pretty soon, journalists turned to her blog for the latest on the issue. By the time the dust settled (and her husband was sick of the subject), her online and in-person activism helped secure the convent a heritage designation.

This is the Internet's greatest gift to the world: a more democratic place to engage with ideas, people and events. But it's up to us to use that power. Pick an issue and own it. Feed your passion with daily posts, tweets and Facebook events. Connect with an online community of like-minded supporters (this will bolster your efforts and remind you that you are not alone). Whether we're tweeting live coverage of the Toronto G20 protests or the earthquake in Haiti, we get back inspiration and information from our fellow Tweeters, Facebook friends and readers. The tools for social change are just at our fingertips and keyboards.

SOLID TIP

TWEET THIS!

- Attending an awareness-raising event? Post it on your Facebook wall, tweet it and invite like-minded friends. If others can't make it, tweet the event live.

- Create a group page for your upcoming event so that attendees can engage with one another long after the event ends.

- When building your readership, Andrea of A Peek Inside the Fishbowl recommends leaving comments on like-minded blogs. This leads the blogger back to your blog. It could gain you one more reader and the attention of that blogger's readers as well.

- Follow change-makers on Twitter and get the latest news right from the horse's mouth. Our favourites include the great humanitarian Mia Farrow as well as *New York Times* columnist Nicholas Kristof.

- Go online at www.metowe.com to post your action and share your thoughts with other like-minded individuals.

·····| READ ALL ABOUT IT! |

62% of North Americans say the Internet has had a major impact for groups shedding light on an issue. Just look at these success stories below.

After launching a YouTube video that depicted the damage of Nestlé's deforesting practices to source palm oil, Greenpeace UK launched a Facebook attack on the company's page. After almost 1.5 million views of the video, over 200,000 emails sent and numerous Facebook comments, Nestlé agreed to change its policy.

*screenshots from greenpeace.org.uk

GO TO PAGE 167 FOR MORE TIPS AND INFORMATION
Source: Mashable.

MENTORING FOR ALL AGES

Jian Ghomeshi

Host and co-creator of the widely popular CBC show, *Q*, Jian Ghomeshi didn't get where he is today without a little guidance from friends and advisors. Today, he's paying it forward by mentoring the young musical prodigy Lights as she navigates the tricky world of entertainment.

THE MOMENT: "About 15 years ago, this veteran newspaper editor became aware of my work. I was in my band Moxy Früvous and I'd written a few op-ed columns for newspapers. So, he took me to lunch. He was really wise and spoke in these Yoda-like proverbs: 'No job is indispensible.' But he has been such an important mentor to me. I talk to him maybe once a year or twice a year now and that consistency over the last 15 years is so important. It feels like he knows me and watches over me."

THE MISSION: "For the first four years I worked with Lights, we had this deal where each month she would make me a CD of songs she had written. Through her mid-teens, each new song she wrote, she was like, 'This is me! This is me!' and it would be like country or death metal. I would say, 'Well maybe it is, but keep going, keep writing.' It's okay to take your time and find your voice, both literally and metaphorically. And that's what happened. She started writing this fusion of pop mixed with '80s new wave and electro sounds. It was unique and very natural feeling. We set up a MySpace site and in six months she had half a million hits and then within a year, more than a million hits. It kind of took off from there and became an online sensation."

THE HABIT: "Whenever I speak to young people, I tell them I can pretty much guarantee, with the exception of a few professional jobs, that you're going to have six, eight, ten different careers in your lifetime. Coming from an Iranian background, there's a lot of pressure to have that professional career. Not that there's anything wrong with being an engineer or a doctor, but there is something wrong if that kid really feels like they have a calling to do something else. As long as they can do education at the same time, why not pursue that path?"

JIAN TAKING A BREAK
AT STUDIO Q

> **"** *Don't be afraid of your own diversity. It's because of my variety of interests that I do my job."*

Day
WANDER LUST

2:00 a.m.
3:00 a.m.
4:00 a.m.
5:00 a.m.
6:00 a.m.
7:00 a.m.
8:00 a.m.
9:00 a.m.
10:00 a.m.
11:00 a.m.
12:00 p.m.
1:00 p.m.
2:00 p.m.
3:00 p.m.
4:00 p.m.
5:00 p.m.
6:0
.m.
0 p.m.
9:00 p.m.
10:00 p.m.
11:00 p.m.
12:00 a.m.

Oh! Canada

Plan A Dream Staycation

FOR THE GIROUARD FAMILY, a mini-vacation is only a transit token away. Their son Louie, now nine, has been in love with trains since he was a toddler. And some extraordinary milestones have happened riding the Toronto transit system, from Louie teaching himself to read with the help of transit maps to an operator letting Louie announce the stations over the PA system to celebrate his third birthday. Instead of rewarding him with a chocolate bar, his parents take him on a bus ride (another interest of his). On these adventures, Louie's mom Sylvia often packs a lunch and the pair escapes on the trains, taking note of everything from the station tiles to the sounds the switches make – all details that go unnoticed by the harried commuters around them.

White sandy beaches, tropical cocktails and crystal blue water: this is what most Canadians think of when imagining their next vacation. Oddly, our own country is frequently overlooked as a destination. Japanese tourists make a pilgrimage to the red roads of Prince Edward Island and Anne of Green Gables' house. Germans crowd our transcontinental trains, *ooh-ing* and *aah-ing* at the Canadian Rockies. European foodies trundle along Quebec backcountry roads, sampling sugar tarts and rabbit terrine. It's fitting, then, that Canadian comic Brent Butt coined the word "staycation" on a *Corner Gas* episode. Canadians need to follow his lead.

After a vacation, the most common complaint is that we're more tired than before we left. A staycation is not only relaxing (no more rushing to and from airports), it trims our carbon footprint and supports the local economy. Most importantly, we can reconnect with our surroundings by visiting a Canadian landmark or just exploring our own backyard. By putting on the tourist hat, locals will treat you like a tourist too, by sharing recommendations, giving directions and becoming more open and engaged. That sense of discovery you normally reserve for exotic locales will transform the streets you call home.

FROM VACATION TO STAYCATION

SOLID TIP

- Make yourself unreachable: turn off your cell, avoid email, tell everyone you'll be unavailable.

- Grab a map of your home province, close your eyes and stick a pin in it. Wherever it lands, take the most scenic routes and stop off at roadside fruit stands, oddball tourist attractions and kitschy diners.

- Pick a street you've never explored on foot and stop at every establishment along the footpath.

- Catch up on the exhibits happening at local museums and art galleries; buy a tourist pass and visit them all.

- Go to that weekly open mic or karaoke you've been meaning to attend.

- Make new discoveries through sport! Look into nearby places to parasail, hang glide, snowshoe or skate.

- Explore the Little Indias and Italys, Chinatowns and Koreatowns that transport you halfway around the world without leaving the city limits.

GET IN TOUCH WITH CANADIANA |

OTTAWA
Pay a visit to the cat man who tends the sanctuary for strays, definitely the quirkiest part of Parliament Hill.

GASPÉ PENINSULA
Rich in cultural history and also an escape to nature, this Quebecois area has boreal forests, Dover-style cliffs, hiking trails and food fit for a proper gourmand.

VANCOUVER
Climb the Grouse Grind, a near vertical hike just outside the city limits.

Discover your **Dream Staycation!**

Welcome to your Neighbourhood!

- Farmer's Market
- Pet Sanctuary
- Fishing hole
- Heritage Home/Museum
- Mountains
- Public Transportation

TORONTO
Ride the Queen Streetcar, the city's most dynamic and longest stretch of streetcar track at 25 kms.

HALIFAX
The new Farmers Market has relocated to the bright and gleaming Pier One, where you can mingle with local farmers and prepare a gourmet picnic lunch. Afterward, visit the old Farmers Market at the Alexander Keith's Brewery where you can take a tour of the almost 200-year-old institution.

EDMONTON
Explore Fort Edmonton park as well as the many other parks that meander through downtown's green valley.

GO TO PAGE 168 FOR MORE TIPS AND INFORMATION

DAY
Wander Lust
3:15 p.m.

See the World

Get Outside Your Comfort Zone

AS DREW DAVIDSON'S HOLIDAY APPROACHED, the 25-year-old writer from small-town Ontario dreamed of visiting the Middle East. The tales of public stonings and suicide bombings on her newsfeed did not deter her: she was convinced there was more to understand. After researching online, she booked a three-week trip to Egypt and Jordan. But when she told others about it (winding catacombs! crumbling pyramids! bustling bazaars!) all she heard were knee-jerk, why-would-you-want-to-go-there reactions. Undeterred, the intrepid young lady set off anyway, travelling across deserts, sleeping under the stars in a Bedouin camp and drifting along the Nile in a felluca (a barge-like boat). Near the end of her trip, she stood on a pier in the town of Aqaba, Jordan where she could see the borders of Jordan, Egypt, Israel and Saudi Arabia. Looking at this cross section, she understood how different each country was and how the term Middle East came no way close to capturing this diversity.

We live in a globalized world in which air travel has opened up the most inaccessible pockets on earth. And yet, finding that authentic, eye-opening experience can be a challenge. To do that, we have to leave our bubble of western amenities. For over a decade, we have spent our summers in Kenya and the place still surprises us. A massive downpour once sent us scurrying for shelter and colliding right into the locals who rushed outside to dance in the rain. Watching them celebrate the end of the drought with such revelry made us question ourselves: why exactly don't we dance in the rain? We took one last look at our dry, clean clothes and ran outside, leaving behind our old preset habits.

SHIFT YOUR VIEW

- Do your due diligence before you set sail. Ask solid questions on what your tour will offer, how the company works with locals and how much free time you will get to explore.

- Search out new culinary adventures while you're there, but check first which stands are hygienic and trustworthy.

- Take a break occasionally from social media by scheduling computer-free chunks of your day.

- Learn as much of the local language as possible. Even knowing a few words can charm the most hardened café owner or bus driver.

- Whenever we visit a new city, we hit up a local café and ask the locals where to eat and what to see and do. It often turns up better recommendations than any travel book.

SOLID TIP

·····| CONSTANT TRAVELLER |

RURAL CHINA
Tour the unspoiled nature and slowed-down pace of China's countryside.

JUNGLES OF COSTA RICA
Pick an eco-lodge to use as your base camp for hiking and white-water rafting trips.

MACCHU PICHU, PERU
Climb over 2,000 metres to the top of this mountain rising out of a tropical rain forest.

THE HOLY LAND
Retrace ancient and sacred sites through Egypt, Syria, Jordan and Israel.

GO TO PAGE 168 FOR MORE TIPS AND INFORMATION

Around the *World*

Go On a Volunteer Trip

FROM THE BLUE SHORES of Vancouver Island to the dusty roads of rural China, Amy Swanton made one great leap forward on her March break. The Grade 11 student from Nanaimo, British Columbia had barely travelled outside North America when she decided to go on a Me to We trip. Picking between trips to Kenya, Ecuador, India, China and the Arizona-Mexico border, she ended up volunteering in the small village of Waer in rural China. As the bus first trundled into the village, Amy was overcome with emotion. Whole families lived in the Canadian equivalent of a shed. Garbage shifted through the streets. Parents farmed cornfields, while children were forced out of school. Surrounded by poverty, Amy still found inspiration in how the community looked out for each other and how she and her classmates could give back, digging the foundation of a new school. Back on Canadian soil, Amy felt uplifted (despite the jet-lag): "It's completely life-changing. All the challenges I face in life now I view with a different perspective," she says. "In reality I can't change the world, but I can start making a difference now."

We take trips to relax and get a tan, explore a city or learn a language. The voluntour experience offers something different: a chance to help others first, and learn about yourself. Hundreds of organizations offer trips tailored to your passion. If you're excited about the environment, you can help collect data on climate change in the Arctic or monitor bird populations in the Amazon. Animal lovers can care for pandas at a sanctuary in China. If ethical food is your bag, go on a low-budget WWOOF (World Wide Opportunities on Organic Farms) excursion across Canada, helping out at family-run, organic farms. Before her voluntour trip, Amy dreamt of a career in computer science. Now she wants to make her life's work about helping others in need, through social work or global studies. For her, China was not only a rad vacation, but a life milestone as well.

GIVE A LITTLE, GET A LOT

- Do what you love and the fun will follow: build your trip around a passion like the environment, sustainable development, literacy and education or wildlife rescue.
- Volunteer trips are not just for youth; adults use it as a career break or a chance to gain new skills.
- Family-friendly volunteer vacations get the kids in on the action, too.
- Keep a journal before, during and after a trip. This will serve as a powerful reminder of your time abroad.
- For those with Internet access while away, start a blog to keep your friends and family up-to-date on your work and activities.
- Exchange addresses with the new friends you meet and keep the connection alive after your trip ends.
- Look into carbon offsetting your flight and minimizing your waste and water use while away.
- After you return, share your story with as many people as possible, such as offering to host a slideshow lunch at work or school where you can share your story with a wider audience.

SOLID TIP

TRIPPING FOR A CAUSE

Every continent in the world has a volunteer opportunity in place.

Amy Swanton poses on the Great Wall

Teaching the children in the village

1,300 volunteers went on 74 trips and logged 145, 600 hours in one year at Me to We.

Helping build a school in rural China

> " *I questioned myself whether I would be up for it, but then you're there and you realize how much you're helping out. You don't think about how hot it is or how heavy the shovel is.*"

GO TO PAGE 169 FOR MORE TIPS AND INFORMATION
Source: Me to We Annual Report 2010, Globe Aware, Planeterra, Gap Adventure.

Tread *Lightly*

Conscientious Jet-Setting

THE PURSUIT OF PLEASURE can be one of the most highly polluting acts in the life of a frequent flyer. Laura Trethewey, an aspiring environmentalist living in Toronto, knew that all too well. She had often taken transatlantic jaunts to her favourite European cities. But with a month off work and a nest egg to crack, she challenged herself to take a vacation that didn't put her values on hold. Sure, boarding a plane meant access to faraway places, but she had the time to take the scenic route. She booked a train ticket to Vancouver from Toronto and brought her bike along as a travel companion. In Winnipeg, Saskatoon and Edmonton, she hopped off and hit the town on her no-cost, no-impact wheels. As the train kept rolling west, she discovered other ways to reduce her footprint. She avoided take-out containers, used a reusable water bottle, reused hotel towels and asked cleaning staff not to change her sheets every day. On her carefree (and car-free) trip across the country, she left the world (as close to) the way she found it.

International air travel has exploded in popularity, with an estimated 935 million jetting off to foreign countries in 2010 compared to 25 million people in the 1960s. This has huge costs for the environment, from untold carbon emissions to rapid development of once-untouched beaches and jungles. But swearing off air travel is not some silver bullet solution, nor is it simple. Tourism is now a major source of jobs in developing countries. Still, why not think twice before you tie on the luggage tags and hit the sky? When you have to fly (it's difficult to paddle the Atlantic for a week's vacation), carbon offset your flight – something that we encourage for all our youth volunteer trips and do regularly for our own flights by planting trees at our tree nursery in Kenya. Take a holistic approach to socially aware travel: choose environmentally friendly options, such as visiting a nature reserve or bird sanctuary, ask before you take pictures and dress to culturally appropriate standards. We're all guests in someone's home as soon as we step outside our doors.

SOLID TIP

LEAVE FOOTPRINTS ONLY

- Choose direct flights and avoid major airports. Planes produce more pollution when taking off and landing. Major airports are often congested, which means your plane is eating up fuel while waiting for landing clearance.

- If you have more time for your trip, think up an adventurous way to get from Point A to Point B rather than planes or cruises.

- Check your tires before starting out on a road trip. Under-inflated tires can increase fuel consumption by 3 percent, and they're also dangerous.

- Avoid aggressive driving. This consumes way more fuel than necessary.

- Carbon offset all your activities with tools such as www.less.ca while away.

CRUISIN' & BRUISIN' THE EARTH

All forms of travel produce some pollution, but cruise ships are among the worst offenders.

Air travel accounts for 3.2% of global pollution

A cruise generates three times as much pollution as a plane trip.

GO TO PAGE 169 FOR MORE TIPS AND INFORMATION
Source: Friends of the Earth.

Pen Pals *Unite*

Stay in Touch Near and Far

SYLVIA KLEINDINST IS A RETIRED ART TEACHER living on the shores of Lake Erie. During the winter, when the roads go unplowed and the lake freezes over, she can go weeks without seeing a soul. But this web-savvy 73 year old is a devoted pen pal and mail artist, who still keeps in touch with her wide network of artists from around the world. After the Berlin Wall came down, a Russian art teacher wrote her, asking to exchange art and lesson plans. Sylvia hesitated. Decades of Cold War propaganda made her somewhat wary of Russians, but she decided to give it a try anyway. Their correspondence showed not only that the pair had heaps in common, it also inspired them to exchange artwork by mail. For the armchair travellers out there, it's a chance to see the world and meet people without leaving the comfort of home.

In the age of Twitter, Facebook, BBM and GChat, writing even a cheque, let alone a letter, has a Shakespearean vibe. The channels of communication have multiplied so vigorously we're more likely to see teens messaging via video games rather than chatting on phones. Some may lament the decline of face-to-face interactions, but our motto is connect by any means possible. We receive correspondence daily from youth in Mexico, Nepal, Indonesia and dozens of other countries. Each letter, email, Facebook post or tweet links us to a stranger who has the power to inspire us with his or her message. It is one powerful lesson in how to empathize with the world.

Twenty years after their correspondence began, Sylvia and her pen pal still talk, albeit these days through Skype or Facebook. This exchange has grown into a rich experiment for both the teachers and their students. Strike up a conversation with a long-lost friend, whether through pen and paper, or email, and encourage family members, especially kids, to do the same. A comforting note could arrive at your darkest hour or you could be the voice of encouragement, cheering someone on from afar. In a post-9/11 world, in which skepticism between the West and Islamic countries has grown and competition between China and the West strains relations, we need to throw open these floodgates of communication more than ever and just connect.

MAKE THAT CONNECTION

SOLID TIP

- Getting snail mail as a kid is always fun. Set up a correspondence between your kids and those of a friend living far away.
- Treat emails to friends and family with the same loving care you would a hand-written letter.
- When travelling, gather names, addresses and emails to keep the correspondence going when you return.
- Pick up a postcard of your favourite home town attraction or site and send it off with a description to a pal far away.
- Be a good Facebook friend: keep up-to-date with pictures or status updates and comment generously on friends' status updates, photos or articles that strike you.

THE TIES THAT BIND

We're connecting with each other more than ever: Just look online!

Facebook is now the second most popular site on the Internet, surpassing YouTube.

Facebook users post **55 million** updates a day and share more than **3.5 billion** pieces of content every week

On 2010-2011 New Year's Eve, Twitter users sent **6,939** tweets per second

GO TO PAGE 170 FOR MORE TIPS AND INFORMATION
Source: *The Economist*, Twitter.

Escape to *Nature*

Keep the Connection

ROB KLEA WAS A LIFELONG ADVENTURER-TURNED-TEACHER who wondered if the troubled teens he taught were missing some real excitement in their lives. Rather than seeking out adventures in the world of crime or drugs, these troubled teens might be looking for an adrenalin rush. And swinging from a towering obstacle course or paddling a canoe through high waves might satisfy their need for speed, and danger. After reading the work of pioneers in the experiential education field, Rob got the opportunity to put these ideas into action. The program he crafted, Citizenship Pathways, takes at-risk youth on adventures in the wild. Over its 16-year history, Rob has seen teenage thugs who have fought in gun battles cower at swinging along the sky-high ropes course, and bad apples blossom during the rigors of a rainy canoe trip. Not every kid is a success story: many come from dysfunctional families and struggle through jail and foster homes regardless. But the success rate (based on whether students are referred back to the program) is high, ranging from 70 to 90 percent. Best of all, Rob runs into former participants who tell him, "I don't remember much about high school, but I remember your program."

A few decades ago, most people had some contact with nature, even if it was car camping a few miles from home. Today, it's possible to avoid the great outdoors completely. And research shows this is a serious problem: our brain chemistry and metabolism work better in nature. Our blood pressure improves and anxiety lessens. As a generation grows up associating nature with dirt, rain or cold, rather than inspiration and excitement, it becomes a commodity to exploit rather than protect. Plus, being out in the wild leaves us with one unforgettable lesson: nature is unpredictable and so is life.

GET OUTSIDE!

- Search out nearby parks and ravines for a quick afternoon hike.

- Robert Louv, the man who literally wrote the book on nature-deficit disorder, suggests letting your backyard grow wild. Small children can still explore a rough patch, turning over rocks and hunting for bugs.

- Don't have time to rough it in the wild? Pitch a tent in the backyard and camp out for a night.

- Learn some roughing-it skills with an organized nature tripper who can plan your adventure and teach you skills to plan your own.

- Spring your kids from soccer practice and a structured schedule. Encourage them to explore nearby woods (give them a cell phone for safety purposes) or enroll them in a daytripping camp that gets them out and exploring with a team and guide.

- Join a hiking or nature walk club.

- Green up your workspace with hanging and potted plants.

- Switch your screensaver image to a view of nature.

- Kids can join Scouts Canada, while adults can volunteer as a leader.

·····|A TREE GROWS IN CALGARY | *...or Toronto, or Montreal, or Vancouver.*

Person living 1,000 m away = visits drop to once a week

Person living 300 m away = visits drop to 2.7 times per week

Person living 50 m or less from the nearest green space = visits green space three to four times a week

Stress increased up to 60%
for those who never visit a garden compared to those who visited often (once or more a week)

photo credits: iStockphoto, Athena's Pix, TheeErin, Zoetnet, Breirrycompton

GO TO PAGE 171 FOR MORE TIPS AND INFORMATION

Source: Swedish University of Agricultural Sciences SLU.w

LEARNING FROM NATURE
Rick Hansen

The man behind the Man in Motion tour has inspired millions of people with his legendary trek around the world. But where does Rick Hansen go when he needs to really get away from it all? To the outdoors, of course, where the consummate woodsman and passionate environmental activist reconnects with nature.

THE MOMENT: "I was very fortunate growing up in Port Alberni, British Columbia, fishing and hiking with my grandfather, father, uncles and cousins. We'd hike through forests, come to the edge of a small lake, climb onto a fallen old-growth tree and fish off it. When I was 10 years old, I was coming down a creek and a monster Fraser River sturgeon jumped out of the river. It was almost bigger than me. I had just never imagined a creature like that before. Years later, we saw a number of Sturgeon wash up on the beach. It was heartbreaking: these fish are great survivors and when a mass amount die in this unexplained way it makes you nervous. I had to find out more and help them, and so I began the Fraser River Sturgeon Conservation Society (FRSCS)."

THE MISSION: "I had my accident coming back from an adventure into the wilderness and afterward it was natural to try to reclaim who I was. At the age of 16, I felt in order to be an ordinary human being I had to be self-reliant and independent. In reality, I had to learn to be interdependent and connected. So, my brother would piggyback me down to the edge of the lake or my friends would lower me down a steep incline or a ledge of rocks and we'd all fish in a raging river. Gaining entry into nature again rekindled my passion and reinforced my values."

THE HABIT: "Every two weeks or so, I'll spend time by the water with friends and family, catching, tagging and releasing fish. My kids and I often spend hours combing the beaches and exploring all the different creatures in tide pools and under rocks. They've come to know that part of the world and they're passionate about it in their own way. At the end of the day, you can't help coming away feeling more relaxed and connected to the planet."

RICK CELEBRATES A BIG HAUL
ON ONE OF HIS TRIPS

" *It's a small world. What we do in Vancouver or
Montreal reaches around the world."*

Evening

HOME
SWEET
HOME

7:00 a.m.
8:00 a.m.
9:00 a.m.
10:00 a.m.
11:00 a.m.
12:00 p.m.
1:00 p.m.
2:00 p.m.
3:00 p.m.
4:00 p.m.
5:00 p.m.
6:00 p.m.
7:00 p.m.
8:00 p.m.
9:00 p.m
10:00 p.
11:00 .m.
a.m.
2:00 a.m.
3:00 a.m.
4:00 a.m.
5:00 a.m.
6:00 a.m.

Behind the *Green Sheen*

Read the Label

GREEN IS ONE EVOCATIVE WORD. It conjures up images of untainted nature, pristine forests and sparkling waterfalls. Oddly we realized this at a home-reno store as we helped our buddy Dave from Edmonton pick out a paint colour for his newborn's nursery. Nearly every product in the store featured a leafy green label; every brand name contained some variant of the word "nature," "pure" or "earth." Marketers are hip to the fact that consumers will drop a few extra bucks for untested and unsupported environmental claims – what's called greenwashing. After Dave shelled out for a light yellow hue of paint, we wondered aloud how truthful the two eco-certifications on the can were. He shot us an annoyed look. After all, he was doing the best for his baby, or so he hoped.

Who can resist a green sales pitch, especially when scary stats say indoor air is up to 1,000 times worse than outdoors, in part polluted by our home cleaners and paints? Just think of Dave's poor baby, forced to inhale chemicals before he can even walk! So we did some online sleuthing on Dave's behalf. One label on his paint was certified by the home reno store itself; the other by the Canadian Paint and Coating Association. Both follow only the minimum lax government regulations on worrisome ingredients, such as volatile organic compounds (or VOCs).

It's not all bad news for the greens who want to go clean. Follow the simple rule of "ask first, buy later." In the case of Dave and his nursery, he eventually returned the original can and bought another certified by Green Seal, an independent, science-based certification. Get familiar with the trusted names (see right) and remember: it's okay to be skeptical, rather than excited, about those "grass is greener" claims.

SOLID TIP

THE GOOD, THE BAD AND THE TOXIC

- Watch out for vague labels, such as "all-natural" (great, so is snake venom), or irrelevant claims like "CFC-free" (the ozone-depleting compound was banned over 30 years ago).

- Buy scent-free wherever possible, as most scents are synthetically created and made using phthalates, a hormone-disrupting chemical.

- "Phosphate-free" labels on laundry detergents are practically useless as most major brands have been free of them for years.

- Take home a natural cleaner and dilute – this will extend the life of the product and also lighten its impact.

LOOK FOR THE LABEL | *Learn the trusted signs of eco-friendly products.*

EcoLogo
A Government of Canada-founded label with some of the most stringent certification standards.
www.ecologo.org

Ecocert
An independent Quebec-based organic certification.
www.ecocertcanada.com

USDA Organic
Organic food and products certified by US Department of Agriculture.
www.ams.usda.gov

EPEAT
A world-wide registry for green electronics.
www.epeat.net

WaterSense
A water-efficiency certification partnered with the US Environmental Protection Agency
www.epa.gov/WaterSense/

FSC (Forest Stewardship Council)
The best certification for guaranteeing sustainably managed forests on paper products.
www.fsccanada.org

GO TO PAGE 171 FOR MORE TIPS AND INFORMATION

Airtight Home

Get an Eco Audit

IT COULD HAVE BEEN THE AFTERMATH OF AN ALIEN ABDUCTION. Giant red tarps covered the front door of Jennifer Atkinson's house, while a huge fan sucked air from the rooms inside, making a strange whirring noise. The back door and windows were also sealed. Rest assured, little green men didn't get the new homeowner. Instead she was nabbed by the urge to perform an eco-audit on her home, which was built in the 1960s.

With good reason. Houses are humongous energy wasters. The coal, gas and electric energy used to heat and cool Canadian homes produce close to half of the country's greenhouse gases. Homes of Jenny's era lose about 20 percent of their energy through doors and windows. She wanted to conquer the drafts before winter hit.

Bob Papadopoulos, an eco-auditor from the non-profit GreenTech Services, let us help out on a draft-hunting mission. A massive fan sucks air from the space and pinpoints the leaky spots. Mini jet streams of air from outside coursed through the rooms. We scrambled through the house and into the attic crawl space, flashlight in one hand, a smoke-puffing wand in the other. While we stalked the drafts, Bob looked for other energy wasters in Jennifer's home.

At the end of the two-hour inspection, he fingered the ancient furnace and water heater for churning out too much energy for the mid-sized home. With a few energy- and cost-saving adjustments (see below), he said Jenny could save up to 30 percent off her energy bill. With government rebates, she could earn back much of the money spent on improvements. Jennifer might not be prepared for alien abductions, but she certainly secured herself an air-tight upgrade on her house.

SOLID TIP

QUICK HOME FIXES

- Do a makeshift energy audit on your home by holding a stick of incense to windows, doors or crawlspaces. If the smoke wavers, you're losing heat.

- Renters can still do quick, cheap changes on their digs, such as stretching a sheet of cellophane over the windows to seal in heat, or buying a new furnace filter (about $20) or a jacket for your hot water heater to keep it extra toasty (about $35).

- Check out alternative energy providers like Bullfrog Power.

- Condo-dwellers can team up with other eco-minded neighbours and approach the building board about sourcing green energy to their building.

- There are hundreds of rebates offered by provincial and territorial governments across the country. You can get $50 off a new 4-litre flushing toilet in Manitoba or $150 off an energy audit in Ontario.

····| KNOW YOUR HOME | *The leaky spots*

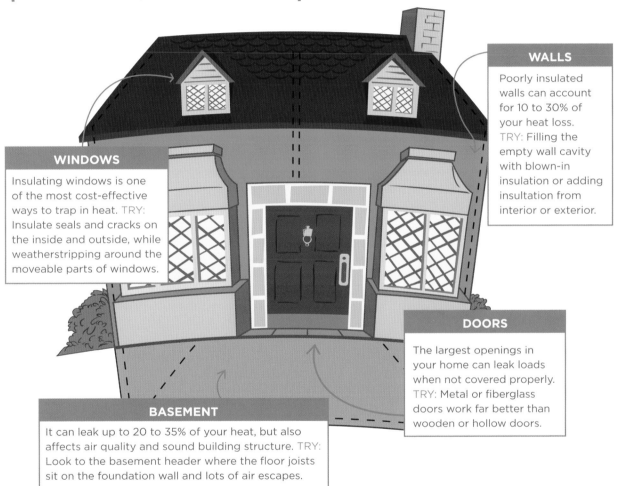

WALLS

Poorly insulated walls can account for 10 to 30% of your heat loss. TRY: Filling the empty wall cavity with blown-in insulation or adding insultation from interior or exterior.

WINDOWS

Insulating windows is one of the most cost-effective ways to trap in heat. TRY: Insulate seals and cracks on the inside and outside, while weatherstripping around the moveable parts of windows.

DOORS

The largest openings in your home can leak loads when not covered properly. TRY: Metal or fiberglass doors work far better than wooden or hollow doors.

BASEMENT

It can leak up to 20 to 35% of your heat, but also affects air quality and sound building structure. TRY: Look to the basement header where the floor joists sit on the foundation wall and lots of air escapes.

DID YOU KNOW?
CANADA RANKS AN EMBARRASSING 27 OUT OF THE 29 DEVELOPED COUNTRIES IN HOME ENERGY USE.

GO TO PAGE 172 FOR MORE TIPS AND INFORMATION

Source: "Keeping the Heat In," published by EcoEnergy and Natural Resources Canada.

Get Out the *Welcome Wagon*

Being a Good Neighbour

TWO ABANDONED CARS can tell one compelling story about the power of community. In 1969, a team of Stanford University psychologists parked two derelict vehicles in the Bronx borough of New York and in Palo Alto, California during its gritty pre-Tech Boom days. The New York team had barely finished setting up its monitoring video equipment, when the first vandals struck. Two days later the car was a husk, stripped of its valuables and vandalized beyond recognition. The Palo Alto car met a very different fate. Not only did a passerby shut its hood when it rained, three different residents called the cops when the scientists attempted to remove the car at the end of the study. The results became the stuff of Psych 101 legend: a sense of anonymity in the Bronx made easy crime even easier, while a tight-knit community in east Palo Alto worked as an informal neighbourhood watch. Years later it continues to blow us away with a simple truth: knowing your neighbours makes for a safer, responsible community.

Keeping up neighbourly relations is not only a cheap alarm system, it fosters a give-and-take symbiosis between you and the people around you – in other words: a community. Canadians have a well-established reputation as being friendly, courteous, and good neighbours. But today, nearly 80 percent of Canadians now live in urban centres and we're not all on cosy terms. Neighbours might share a wall or a fence, but for many that's about it. Personally, with our busy schedules, and many late nights at the office or in airports, we confess we struggle to know our neighbours. But we're trying. After all, if you acquaint yourself with the people next door, you're more likely to respect each other's requests for quiet during a floor-stomping party or for patience during a massive reno. Who knows, you might even find yourself borrowing a cup of sugar (no, it doesn't just happen in some *Pleasantville* suburb).

GET TO KNOW THE JONESES

- First things first: try smiling or nodding hello to familiar faces around the neighbourhood.
- For the increasing numbers of us living in buildings, host meet-and-greets in a communal area.
- Join the ranks of your neighbourhood association and get to know the locals.
- Bring by a bottle of wine or drop off a welcome card to a newcomer.
- Walk your kids to school or the park, an easy place to mingle with other nearby families.
- If your neighbours are away, clear away conspicuous signs like left-out recycling or garbage bins to a less obvious space.
- Band together with the locals to hold a street party.
- Start a dog walking group to help take turns walking the pooch.
- After finishing mowing your lawn, try pushing the mower an extra minute and do the next house's lawn too.
- Coordinate a street garage sale and invite neighbours to contribute. The money earned can go toward a backyard barbecue or block party.
- Start a neighbourhood watch program.

..... | PROFILE: COMMUNITY BUILDER |

PHOTOGRAPHY BY JOSH SAM

Rory "Gus" Sinclair
former president of the Harbord Village Residents' Association

By day, he's a general contractor. By night and pretty much every other hour of the day, he's the local superhero of his downtown Toronto neighbourhood. Meet Gus, 65 years old, who lives by the motto that "every time you shake hands with a neighbour, you make the community stronger." He's lived on the block for 20 years now, exchanging hellos, taking care of the neighbours' pets and volunteering on the residents' association. But his favourite way of making new friends is via their stomach. "I love making bread. I'm up to 25,000 loaves now, "he says. "My neighbours love it, it's my recipe, so when I have some extra loaves, I take it over to the nearest neighbour and say, 'from me to you.'"

"*Every time you shake hands with a neighbour, you make the community stronger.*"
RORY "GUS" SINCLAIR

GO TO PAGE 172 FOR MORE TIPS AND INFORMATION

Mop *Softly*

Cleaning with Alternative Home Cleaners

WHAT KID CAN TURN A FAILED ATTEMPT to avoid cleaning duty into an aced science project? In our house, Marc was known for his uncanny ability to avoid chores. If a toilet needed plunging or a lawn mowing, his mission was to go missing. Or at least sweet talk his way out of the task. One time Mom cornered him in the bathroom with a mop and cleaning products. While desperately thinking how to get out of cleaning the toilet, Marc noticed scary labels on the cleaning products: flammable, corrosive and poisonous. They looked unsafe for anyone to handle, let alone a kid. Marc pointed this out to Mom. Although she figured it was just an excuse to escape, how could she argue with his alarm?

Although Marc was first motivated by a healthy aversion to cleaning duty, his cause for concern was real. A typical cleaning product can release around 40 contaminants into the air, many linked to cancer, asthma and a host of other health problems. Green products fare only slightly better, letting off a quarter of the contaminants that conventional products do. And the damage doesn't stop there. Think of the Great Lakes or Athabasca River choked with drain cleaner or toilet bowl washer.

But what was the solution? It wasn't until Marc got a peek inside our grandmother's gleaming cupboards in her home in Windsor that he discovered that tried-and-true, non-toxic ingredients – and a little bit of elbow grease – worked just as well. Our Mimi relied on everyday items, such as vinegar, borax, baking soda, salt and hydrogen peroxide. Armed with research and recipes, Marc set up a booth at a science fair to promote alternative home cleaners over store-bought stuff. It was a hit. By using these one-step recipes, you're not only avoiding the harsh chemicals, you're saving serious cash too: some $200 to $300 a year! As for Marc and cleaning duty, he was eventually forced to scrub that toilet, albeit with Mimi's cleaning concoctions instead.

THE GENTLER WAY

- Using softer home-made cleaners means your kids can easily lend a hand.
- Combine castile soap with a few drops of your favourite essential oils for an easy washing-up fluid for dishes. Note: this doesn't work in a washing machine, only for hand-washing.
- Mix together one cup of water with 1/8 cup of liquid castile soap, a 1/2 tsp of baking soda and one tablespoon of vinegar for a fabric cleaner.
- Reuse old spray bottles and containers to make your own products.
- Rip up old T-shirts or towels instead of using wasteful disposable wipes, mops and dusters.
- An all-purpose mix of half vinegar and half water works well on most surfaces.
- Not ready to throw out all your old products? Dilute with water to ease the harshness and extend their life cycles.

SOLID TIP

CREATE YOUR OWN CLEANERS

TRY OUT MARC'S SPECIAL HOME CLEANERS*
COURTESY OF GRANDMA MIMI

BAKING SODA
a natural deodorizer that also eats up grease

LEMON JUICE
works as a cleaner, deodorizer and cuts grease

WHITE VINEGAR
works as a cleaner, deodorizer and cuts grease

SALT
disinfectant and abrasive

CASTILE SOAP
a gentle vegetable-based soap

BORAX (also known as sodium borate)
a disinfectant and cleaner

HYDROGEN PEROXIDE
disinfectant and works as non-chlorine bleach

*See full recipes in the resource guide.

GO TO PAGE 173 FOR MORE TIPS AND INFORMATION
Source: *Make Your Place* by Raleigh Briggs (Microcosm Press).

Share Your Home

Enjoy Community Space

TO THE UNINFORMED EYE (our neighbours!), the early days of Free The Children probably looked like a bunch of kids hanging out at our parents' house. Sure we shot hoops and ate pizza, but mostly we fought child labour. Even with all our passion, without that living room as our ad hoc headquarters, we quite literally would have been outside in a tree house, making calls on a tin can phone. Free The Children owes its existence, in many ways, to our mom and dad.

Sometimes the lack of free space can be all that stands in the way of great things happening. Many non-profits start with nothing but an idea and a place for people to gather. The Anchor Archive Zine Library in Halifax started in the home of two activists, who invited the community to drop by on weekend afternoons and read their zine collection. It's just that easy: make the space available and people will come. With the exploding size of modern homes we have more space than ever. A new home today measures 1,389 square feet – or the average size of a three-bedroom apartment – larger than in the 1950s, while occupancy has shrunk from 3.3 people in the 1960s to 2.6 today. Give a second life to those rooms where you ditch untouched snowshoes or extra chairs.

Not every donated room turns into an international charity. But think of the possibilities: a room can house a craft night, a weekly salon or an indie movie theatre. Pick your passion, then poll your pals on interest. Donate a room to upstart non-profit groups or organizations you're interested in supporting. It's the simplest way to bring community home.

SOLID TIP

EXPAND YOUR SPACE

- Donate an advertising spot on your website, Facebook, Twitter page or blog to an organization or group hoping to raise its profile.

- For cottage owners out there, offer your rustic spot to a family in need of a little rest and relaxation.

- Lend tent space by offering your camping equipment to a youth group, such as Scouts Canada.

- For young parents, make a gathering space for coffee and parenting advice. Invite local parenting gurus to give talks, or teachers to do informal yoga lessons.

HOME MAKEOVER | *Look at all the ways to donate your space!*

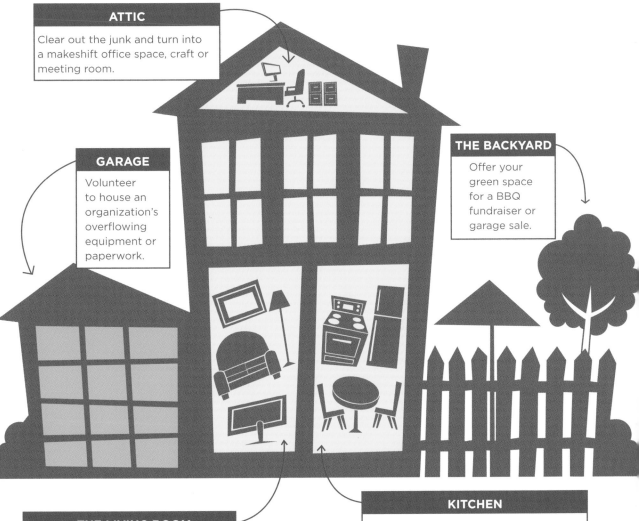

ATTIC

Clear out the junk and turn into a makeshift office space, craft or meeting room.

GARAGE

Volunteer to house an organization's overflowing equipment or paperwork.

THE BACKYARD

Offer your green space for a BBQ fundraiser or garage sale.

THE LIVING ROOM

This could double as the headquarters for a budding social activism group.

KITCHEN

Lend your cooking equipment to support a bake-sale fundraiser.

GO TO PAGE 173 FOR MORE TIPS AND INFORMATION

GREENING THE HOMESTEAD
Anne Murray

This snowbird, who's serenaded Canadians for decades, hardly needs an introduction. But many residents of her home and native land might not know about Anne Murray's long-time love for the environment. When she's not singing songs or winning awards, Anne takes some simple steps to green her home in Toronto.

THE MOMENT: "In the 1970s, when I started touring, I remember very clearly going to Little Rock, Arkansas. The city was littered from one end of the city to the other. I had never seen anything like it. Now, it was spring, granted, so they hadn't gotten around to cleaning it, but it was an eye opener for me. How fortunate I was to be living in Canada! I grew up in Nova Scotia where everything is pristine. Even in Toronto, the reputation of the city worldwide is how clean it is. As soon as people started talking about the environment, I jumped on the bandwagon. It just made so much sense to me."

THE MISSION: "Very early on, I stopped using paper napkins, paper towels and plastic. People would roll their eyes at me. Even my own mother would say, 'Oh, Anne, don't be silly.' In the mid-'80s, I bought these mesh bags and took them to the grocery story. The cashiers used to give us the toughest time until finally I had to go to the manager and have a real chat with him. And it never happened again."

THE HABIT: "The first thing to do is to go out and buy a drawer full of Tupperware. Get rid of all the [plastic] baggies and Swiffers, too. My house is really clean and I don't use any of that stuff. My daughter always complains that it's too cold in my house and she can't stay there. I tell her to "bundle up!" I also stopped using pesticides on my lawn years ago. I do cold washes and use environmentally safe detergent and cleaners. I have an organic garden in the backyard with every vegetable you could imagine: beans, peas, radishes, tomatoes. We freeze it all and eat it in the winter."

ANNE TENDING HER GARDEN
IN TORONTO

" *Sometimes I seem a bit preachy but I don't mean to be. I'm just passionate about this and I think people should pay attention.* "

Evening
FOOD
FIGHT

8:00 a.m.
9:00 a.m.
10:00 a.m.
11:00 a.m.
12:00 p.m.
1:00 p.m.
2:00 p.m.
3:00 p.m.
4:00 p.m.
5:00 p.m.
6:00 p.m.
7:00 p.m.
8:00 p.m.
9:00 p.m.
10:00 p.m.
11:00 p.m.
12:00 a.m.
1:00 a.m.
3:00 a.m.
4:00 a.m.
5:00 a.m.
6:00 a.m.

Happy *Meals*

Bringing Back Communal Dining

IN OUR EXPERIENCE, THERE ARE TWO TYPES OF PEOPLE at conferences: those who conspicuously network and those who naturally connect. At the World Economic Forum 15 years ago, the room was full of glad-handing and chit-chat, but Keith Ferrazzi stood out. The 30-something chief marketing officer of Starwood Resorts knew everyone in the room, asked after family members, remembered someone's bad back, another's hang-gliding hobby. We later asked him how he managed to bring this personal touch to the stale conference space. "It's simple," he said, adding, "I never eat alone." And then he promptly invited us to dinner. By taking attendees to a personal meal, Keith not only made business connections, but friends. Over the years, so many people have asked him the same question we did that he later wrote a book called, appropriately, *Never Eat Alone*.

That a good meal goes hand-in-hand with great conversation should be no secret. The presence of food lightens the atmosphere: we tell stories, exchange ideas and speak our minds. And yet, sharing a meal is often the first thing cut from our busy schedules. Instead we eat at our computers, cramming the keys with gunk, or in our cars, which become our personal composter on wheels. The family dinner is endangered in many households because parents and kids eat at different times or even in different rooms. If, by some scheduling miracle, everyone does gather for a meal, gadgets ring, buzz and ping.

The value of eating together is tricky to quantify, but not impossible. It strengthens community ties, improves conversation skills and even helps weight loss. There are numerous ways to lure friends and family to the table – and we're not just talking about inspired place settings! Ferrazzi's personal tips include simple but important gestures, like sending out personally written invitations or inviting the kids' same-age friends to the table. The locavore and slow food movements have taken a long, hard look at what's on our plates, but what about who's sitting at the table? Shake up your routine and make conversation and company the main course of your next meal.

SOLID TIP

KEITH FERRAZZI'S PRO TIPS TO SUCCESSFUL DINNERS

- Use a long, thin table so that guests can easily engage without straining to hear the conversation.
- Ask friends beforehand for suggestions on people they would like to meet at a dinner party. Arrange a seating plan to facilitate a conversation between new-found friends.
- Make lighting one shade brighter than a romantic date for a warm and inviting space.
- Games like Table Topics can turn the stuff of typical dinner conversations into compelling chatter and help encourage more shy members of the table to speak up.

····| ALL TOGETHER AT THE TABLE |

It takes your stomach
20 minutes
to know it's full.

Plowing through a meal alone means you'll miss the clues your stomach is sending and keep eating beyond satiation.

Studies have shown that kids who eat regular family dinners are **less likely to abuse alcohol and drugs.**

Eating even one meal outside the home a day

takes a toll on a teen's body, decreasing her intake of calcium, iron, Vitamin C and thiamine.

IKEA®
It's called the Ikea effect:

scientists have proven that when you make something yourself
– say a Billy bookcase or a Poang armchair – you appreciate it more!
Ergo, that home-cooked meal will taste better too

Source: *Wired* Magazine, OECD, U.S. Public Health Service, *Canadian Living* and *Reader's Digest*.

Photos ©iStockphoto, ©austincvan, ©reverendo, ZIM, xinou bao

Going the Distance

Eat Local

STOP US IF YOU'VE HEARD THIS ONE: celebrity chef Jamie Oliver walks into a classroom and asks a group of first-graders to identify a line-up of vegetables. A tomato is called a potato, an eggplant a pear and yes, french fries, are considered vegetables. We heard this story at a conference afterparty where we met the famous Brit himself. It entertained at the time, but it also got us thinking, would we have fared much better at that age? Growing up in the Toronto suburb of Thornhill, we never saw a farm. Meat came tidily packaged in plastic wrap; fruit and vegetables were unloaded from the trunk. Did a strawberry fall from a tree? Did celery get dug up from the ground? Who knew?

Some realities have to be faced, like the fact that Canada is a cold, hard land eight months of the year and not exactly bursting with fruit flavour in the middle of January. But doesn't it seem odd that your New Zealand lamb or Kobe beef is better travelled than you are? Canadian imports from places like China are on the rise , which means the odometer on our food is ticking up also. The average food mileage on a meal made from a mainstream grocery store clocks in at 2,400 km. But movements like the "100-mile diet" are changing all of that, with people planting backyard gardens, jarring their own preserves and digging up root cellars. For the less pioneering of us, taking simple steps like reading the origin label on your food, saying no to those from far-flung places, shopping at the farmers market and supporting local shops helps reduce the farm-to-plate journey.

GARDEN STATE

No need to bust out the backhoe just yet. Try these simple ways to trim your food mileage:

- The Green Food Box program available in dozens of communities across Canada, sells local, organic produce for cheap in re-usable green boxes.

- There are over 200 food co-ops in Canada, many of which specialize in providing local and organic food options to its members.

- There are over 550 farmers markets across Canada. Visit one!

- Start a windowsill herb garden for fresh flavouring year-round. Hang these herbs to dry or blend them with olive oil to keep longer.

- Buyer beware: just because your food comes from a nearby farm doesn't make it organic. Go the extra mile and ask whether it's pesticide free.

- Canada is one big country, so the "Made in Canada" label can still mean an apple travelled over 3,000 km. Look for a label specific to your province or territory on produce and goods.

- Watch out: "Imported by" followed by a local company doesn't mean the product was made anywhere close to you.

- Freeze summer berries, sun dry or dehydrate tomatoes or store root vegetables in cool places in your home.

SOLID TIP

WHERE WE GET OUR FOOD

A groundbreaking study by the advocacy group Food Share clocked in the CO_2 emissions from locally-grown and shipped-in produce to Toronto.

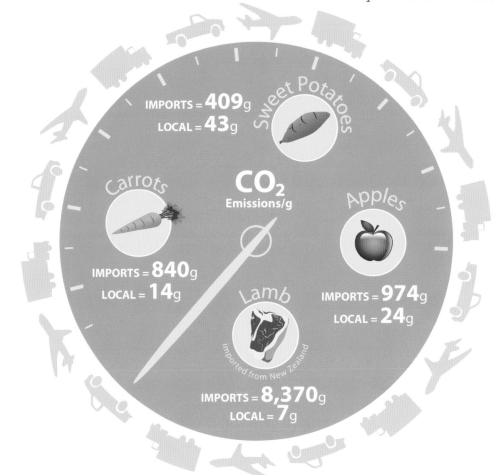

Sweet Potatoes
IMPORTS = **409**g
LOCAL = **43**g

CO_2
Emissions/g

Carrots
IMPORTS = **840**g
LOCAL = **14**g

Apples
IMPORTS = **974**g
LOCAL = **24**g

Lamb
imported from New Zealand
IMPORTS = **8,370**g
LOCAL = **7**g

DID YOU KNOW?
HOMEGROWN PRODUCE IS IN THE PITS. BRITISH COLUMBIA, OUR MOST ABUNDANT OF PROVINCES, USED TO BOAST 200 ONION GROWERS AND IS NOW REDUCED TO THREE. THE CATTLE SECTOR SHRUNK 25% IN ONE YEAR AND THE TREE FRUIT INDUSTRY HAS LOST 100 MILLION POUNDS OF FRUIT OVER THE LAST 15 YEARS.

GO TO PAGE 174 FOR MORE TIPS AND INFORMATION
Source: FoodShare.

Food Waste *Flaws*

Finish Your Plate

NO DESSERT UNTIL YOU FINISH YOUR VEGETABLES. Don't you know there are starving kids in Africa? Oh, the parental admonitions levelled at an 8 year old refusing to finish her plate. We heard them too and it's taken two decades to understand that eating up our spinach is not just sound advice for Popeye wannabes. We throw away 40 percent of our food supply every year through restaurants, supermarkets or at home. That's a whole lot of rubbery oatmeal and wilted lettuce! And rotting food doesn't simply fill up space once it reaches the landfill. It continues to pollute, decomposing and releasing methane – a powerful greenhouse gas – long after you've tossed it.

Believe it or not, the food industry is wasteful itself. It doesn't make much business sense, but western countries such as Canada produce 200 percent more food than we actually need. This abundance makes us take food for granted. There's that tub of yogurt with a mould farm growing on top or the mushy kale rotting in the crisper. Canada's growing curbside collection programs force us to confront our food waste problem, but scraps still get thrown away. Rather than using the food in our fridge, we go out for dinner. Or we might get seduced by a fancy new recipe and throw out yesterday's leftovers. Breaking bad habits means getting re-connected with your fridge and being creative in the kitchen while enjoying awesome perks like saving money and waste.

SOLID TIP

BECOME A FOOD WASTE SAINT

- Bring a list! You'll be less inclined to impulse buy.

- Avoid buying flats of over-ripe strawberries or two-for-one yogurt tub deals. Unless you have an exact recipe in mind, much of this excess food will end up in the trash.

- Revamp portion sizes by starting small and going back for seconds later.

- Clean and cut up produce before putting it in the fridge – you're much more likely to use it this way.

- If you buy meat in bulk, remove the original flimsy packaging and rewrap in plastic wrap and seal in a sturdy freezer bag.

- Do the sniff taste test: yogurt and eggs are often still edible past their best-before dates. Obey time stamps on cold cuts, sushi, chopped salad and soft or semi-soft cheeses.

- With big-batch recipes, divide it up and freeze half for later.

- Tips: use blackened bananas in banana bread; mushy tomatoes in pasta sauce; stale bread in French toast or crushed into bread crumbs; potatoes turned into mashed used in shepherd's pie; leftover pasta in an omelet or strata; save cheese rinds to add to soup stock.

WHERE OUR FOOD GOES

It's often easier and cheaper to throw food away than, say, not make it in the first place. This means waste is actually part of the food system. Just look around...

UNPROFITABLE

- Beauty standards keep 25 to 40% of produce off our aisles (ever wonder why you've never seen a gnarled carrot or super-size-me potato?)
- From 2004 to 2010, Canada shipped 400 truckloads of waste to the U.S. every day.
- Western countries now produce 200% more food than we need.
- 2% of North America's total energy usage (or 350 million barrels of oil) could be saved by simply not tossing out food.

GO TO PAGE 175 FOR MORE TIPS AND INFORMATION
Source: StatsCan, *Chatelaine* and *Maclean's*.

THE FAMILY MAN

Sam **Roberts**

Over a decade ago, Montreal's JUNO-award winning Sam Roberts shot to the top of the charts with his hit single "Brother Down." Today, he works hard to balance the rock star lifestyle with that of proud pop to three tots.

THE MOMENT: "Sometimes it feels like society is getting further and further away from the simple kinds of interactions: communities are less important; the family is disintegrating and people are pulling away from each other. These days, even having two kids means you're above average. At three kids, we're practically a nineteenth century farming family. But I grew up as one of four boys and I've always wanted a large family. I guess I'm old-fashioned that way. I get nostalgic about things like family dinners, teaching my kids to ice skate or playing music together."

THE HABIT: "My wife and I have been together for a long time, so our relationship has always included touring in some way. Now, we're trying to include our whole family. My kids have grown up with this, but it's still not easy for them or for me. The band used to tour three months or four months at a time without ever setting foot in the door at home. That just doesn't happen anymore. Every couple of weeks, I make sure to come home, reconnect around the dinner table with family and some great food."

THE MISSION: "My family has become a huge motivating force for me. Every show has to be that much better than the last or I feel like I'm letting them down."

SAM ROBERTS KNOWS THE
VALUE OF TIME WITH FAMILY

66 *If I'm going to be spending time away from my family doing something that I feel is really important, then I better do it well."*

Evening
FAM
JAM

8:00 a.m.
9:00 a.m.
10:00 a.m.
11:00 a.m.
12:00 p.m.
1:00 p.m.
2:00 p.m.
3:00 p.m.
4:00 p.m.
5:00 p.m.
6:00 p.m.
7:00 p.m.
8:00 p.m.
9:00 p.m.
10:00 p.m.
11:00 p.m.
12:0
.m.
:00 a.m.
3:00 a.m.
4:00 a.m.
5:00 a.m.
6:00 a.m.

The *Art* of Family Traditions

Do it Together

WHEN CORINNE IMPEY WAS GROWING UP in Colborne, Ontario, her family was close with their elderly next-door neighbours, Tom and Frances Cochrane. One Christmas the task of putting up the tree became too much for the couple, so Corinne and her family snuck in while the couple was out (each had keys to the other's house) and put up a little pine tree, complete with hand-made decorations. Tom later called to thank them for the "Charlie Brown" tree, the scrawniest thing he'd ever seen. The next Christmas eve, after the Cochranes had gone to bed, Corinne's family built a snowman wearing a trucker hat just like Tom's outside their living room window. These small acts grew into a holiday tradition. It didn't feel like Christmas without doing something nice for the Cochranes.

Whether it's a special Sunday night dinner, a weekend nature walk, or volunteering as a family, these become the memories that get us choked up years later. Studies show that the earlier children learn to help others, the more likely they are to act charitably throughout their lives. When building a family tradition, try to incorporate a socially conscious angle. Kick off every summer with a fundraising lemonade stand. Pick a social topic to discuss over dinner. Tackle the spring cleaning chores together, collecting useful items to donate to charity. Put an extra present under the Christmas tree each year to donate to a child in need. These acts seem small, but over time they grow into something mighty.

THE FAMILY THAT VOLUNTEERS TOGETHER, STAYS TOGETHER

- Do a neighbourhood clean-up with the kids, bagging leaves or shoveling snow for anyone on the block who needs the extra help.

- Turn a holiday or birthday gift into a socially conscious project, getting kids to research an organization with the promise of donating a gift to their favourite.

- Take a nature walk as a family, either to the nearest park or on an annual camping trip. Quiz one another on the animals, plants and sights you see along the way.

- Prepare a weekly meal together as a family, making a little extra to bring to a friend or family member who is strapped for time.

- Know a couple of friends with parenting responsibilities? Offer to babysit so they can go on a date night.

TEAM FAMILY

39% of volunteers had parents who volunteered

Corinne shares some of her family pictures

26% of volunteers get involved as a family

42% of kids who were active in school government volunteered

GO TO PAGE 175 FOR MORE TIPS AND INFORMATION
Source: Imagine Canada, *Journal of Adolescent Research.*

EVENING
Fam Jam
7:15 p.m.

Material World

Raise Socially Conscious Kids

KIDS ARE NOT BORN with some innate need for smart phones and game consoles. Nor are they made to shop until they drop. Today's savvy advertisers excel at targeting the insecurities of tweens and teens. But that old annoying rhyme our parents used to sing still rings true: "Gimme, gimme never gets, don't you know your manners yet?" That's not to say we were immune back then. Growing up in the well-heeled Toronto suburb of Thornhill, our parents made sure we lacked for nothing. But the line between "need" and "want" definitely blurred at times. (For example, did we really "need" those $150 jeans?) Rather than give us what we demanded, our parents took the opposite tactic. Mom took us shopping at second hand stores and helped us hunt for flea market finds. She also threw in a dose of reality by volunteering with us at food banks and introducing us to the homeless. If we truly needed that new pair of jeans, she gave us the cash and let us decide if the pants were worth the price. Sometimes we splurged, sometimes we saved and sometimes we gave the cash away.

Science has proven that helping others is a far better buy. After lending a hand or giving to charity, we get what's called a natural "helper's high" that engages the same parts of the brain that experiences pleasure. Studies have also shown that "materialistic" kids are less likely to give back to their world by recycling, riding a bike or engaging in other socially conscious acts. Next time you yearn to break the bank or your child begs for something, check yourself. Refraining from the splurge just might make you and your kids happier in the long run.

SOLID TIP

CURING THE GIMMIES

- Take the Buy Nothing Day challenge in late November, right before the infamous Black Friday shopping day, by going one day without making a single purchase.

- Sit down with your kids and watch a few ads with them, asking questions like what else the commercial purports to be selling, besides the product. Fame? Beauty? Popularity? Family togetherness?

- Instead of giving presents, give presence. Be there for your kids in times of trouble and you can quell that need for more stuff.

- Advocate against advertising in schools.

- Try restricting TV and Internet consumption to an hour or less a day.

KIDS AND ADVERTISING | *A dangerous combo for some...*

Before the ages of 4 and 5, children cannot consistently differentiate ads from television programs.

Over 75% of young kids believe product-centred games are "just games." By Grade 4, awareness of the advertising rises to 18% and then 31% in Grade 11.

Children younger than 7 or 8 cannot understand the persuasive intent of commercials.

GO TO PAGE 176 FOR MORE TIPS AND INFORMATION

Source: American Psychological Association, Media Awareness Network.

Gift + *Passion* = Better World
Learn the Equation for Change

MEET THE PRECOCIOUS SCARLET PAGE, all of eight years old and absolutely certain she wants to be a chef, so don't tell her any different. She loves helping out in the kitchen; her allowance goes toward treating her friends to high tea at Ottawa's Chateau Laurier and her birthday present is a meal at the latest restaurant – hardly ever McDonald's. But her eye is not only on her own prize. She also wants to help others by organizing lemonade stands and bake sales for her favourite causes. At her elementary school in Ottawa, Scarlet found a group of like-minded chums who formed Souper Soups – a project that raises money for charity by selling soup. The group also grew with the help of the charity The Learning Partnership. Besides a few parents on hand (and a few inspired teachers) to ensure fingers are not grated in the school's small kitchen, it's a kid-led initiative, including the sales force and cookbook design team. The squad of chefs have sold dozens of litres of soup (mostly to hungry teachers) and raised hundreds of dollars for charity. Carrot ginger or wonton anyone?

Whether Scarlet knows it or not, she's harnessed one of the most powerful tools for change. It's a simple equation we like to call Gift + Passion = Better World. Broken down, this means combining what you're good at with what you care about to make the world a better place. At Free The Children, we see this equation every day. Take Jonas – a natural public speaker with a passion for clean water and irrigation pumps. After giving speeches at his rotary club, he raised $500 for a Kenyan village's new pump. Then there's Maggie, a serious dancer, who created a successful show that raised $1,200 for charity. Parents can get involved too, helping a child identify their special talent or gift, then brainstorming ways to link it to passion and change. Or even by being a silent but strong supporter, offering a hug when a challenge arises or helping out with a carpool.

ON THE WAY TO CHANGING THE WORLD

- A gift of the gab, a killer sense of humour, graphic design skills, computer programming savvy, organizational zest. Everyone has a talent, even if it remains untapped. What's yours?

- Fact-find to locate a cause: read the paper, pay attention to your neighbours and neighbourhood, keep an ear to the ground.

- Once a cause is identified, research the subject thoroughly.

- Brainstorm what type of contribution a cause needs most: fundraising, awareness or volunteer time.

- Tell others about the cause, whether that's through word of mouth or online.

- Build a team: engage other like-minded pals to help pursue the goal.

- Couple your cause with a fun hang-out. Order pizza in for an information session or pair an activity with a fundraiser, like, say, a bowl-a-thon or bake-off.

....|DO THE MATH | *Add your skills and passion to a great cause.*

GIFT

Good Listener

Physical Strength

Writing

Language

ACT

Volunteer at a peer helpline; be there for your pals

Shovel an elderly neighbour's drive; take out the trash

Start a Facebook page devoted to covering local issues

Offer to help translate for a new immigrant family

GO TO PAGE 177 FOR MORE TIPS AND INFORMATION

Random Act of Kindness

Pay it Forward

LOOK CLOSER. The paperback that was left on the backseat of the bus is not just a forgotten tome: it's actually the physical manifestation of a favour passed forward. The BookCrossings program, and its website that allows people to label, share and track their released books around the world, started over a decade ago and is still going strong. From preteens dropping off novels at the community centre, to elderly ladies leaving behind paperbacks at the local café, the program lets us open our personal libraries to the world. Close to eight million books are now travelling around the world, finding their ways into the hands of unwitting bookworms. And the best part is that the finder has the chance to pay the favour forward: they can turn around and release the found book back into the wild. Canadians love this selfless exchange: our active book sharing community comes in sixth out of the 132 countries that participate.

Science proves that it feels good to give and receive (see the graphic, right). People are more likely to do someone else a good turn after experiencing some luck themselves. In a landmark study, a huge majority of people (84 percent) who discovered a dime left in a pay phone (back when people still used pay phones), were more likely to help an elderly man picking up dropped paper. Only 4 percent of those who hadn't found the dime stopped to help. Considering that a mere 10 cents can prompt us to pay it forward, we should all try to spread a little goodwill. Cast off those laws of reciprocity and do a good deed for a complete stranger or pal, unasked.

THE MILK OF HUMAN KINDNESS

- Donate a book to the BookCrossings program (www.bookcrossing.com).
- Brainstorm a list of gestures that would make your day, from a nice compliment to a friendly email check-in from a friend or family member.
- Let someone in a rush go ahead of you in line.
- Help someone with a heavy load if you're going the same way.
- Ask the person behind you at the coffee counter what they're ordering and buy them a drink.
- Shovel your neighbour's driveway.
- Surprise a sick friend with soup.
- Return a too-busy friend's library books or videos for them.

....| ONE GOOD TURN DESERVES ANOTHER |

Studies show that altruism is not just some do-gooding emotion. It has many helpful benefits for the do-gooder as well.

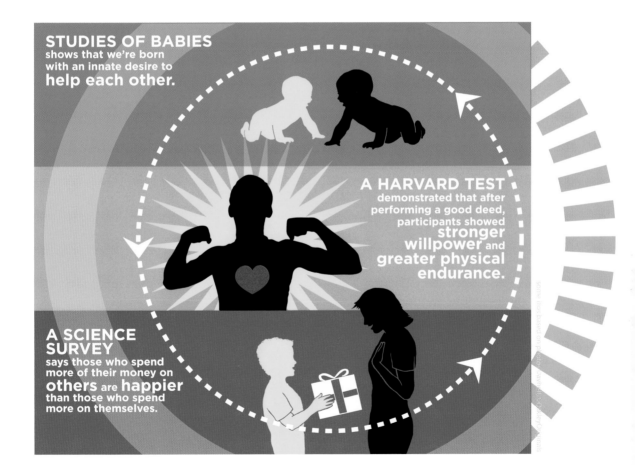

STUDIES OF BABIES shows that we're born with an innate desire to **help each other.**

A HARVARD TEST demonstrated that after performing a good deed, participants showed **stronger willpower** and **greater physical endurance.**

A SCIENCE SURVEY says those who spend more of their money on **others** are **happier** than those who spend more on themselves.

GO TO PAGE 177 FOR MORE TIPS AND INFORMATION

Source: *Science* Magazine, *The Harvard Crimson*, *Why We Cooperate* by Dr. Michael Tomasello (MIT Press).

Children's Books with *Substance*

Finding the Power of Stories

WHITHER THE LOWLY BUT LOVEABLE BOOKWORM? No longer teetering out of libraries beneath the weight of towers of books, many of us have abandoned libraries for video games and social media sites. But our inner bookworm thrives on stories of falling through rabbit holes or crawling through enchanted cupboards. Back in the day, we both loved reading the Hardy Boys tales, while Craig treasured his leather-bound edition of *King Arthur: Tales From the Round Table*. But we lose much more than a rich inner life when we give up reading. Society loses, too. Proficient adult readers tend to be more civically engaged, voting and volunteering close to 30 percent more than non-readers. Kids with books in the home consistently score higher grades across a range of subjects, from civics to science. They soak up information about their world better than the leading brand of paper towel soaks up spills. We can quench that thirst with books that impart meaningful messages.

Jason Martorino, a teacher at an inner-city school in Scarborough, a suburb of Toronto, is always bringing dynamic kid fare into his classroom. He challenges his Grade 4 students daily with universally appealing stories of social justice from books, graphic novels and real life. These provoke discussions with 9 and 10 year olds grappling with the reasons for child slavery or climate change. One discussion about Iqbal Masih, the freed child slave who became an activist, prompted a girl to ask if she had a role in his story. Could the carpet the kids sat cross-legged on in Jason's class be made by a child slave? What steps could she take if it was?

Our parents, both teachers, used Mark Twain's *Adventures of Huckleberry Finn* to gently draw out discussions on empathy and ethics. Why did Huck choose the harder path of concealing his friend Jim when he could have given him up for a reward? Sometimes there are no easy answers, but we shouldn't shy away from challenging kids with tough questions that books can provoke.

GET YOUR READ ON

- Get your child a library card as early as possible. It teaches responsibility and opens up a world of books to borrow.

- Read the same books as your kids, so you can ask questions about plot, characters and meaning. This can open up discussion on moral messages.

- Subscribe to your child's favourite magazines. Your child will love receiving his or her own mail, while the reading materials that arrive will become more exciting.

- Ask friends and family to give your child books as gifts.

- Bring along books on tape for car rides. For young children, try sing-a-long stories that can turn a long drive into a pow wow.

- Encourage your child to create a "reading nook" in your home by filling it with comfy pillows and a collection of books.

....| BRAIN FOOD, NOT BRAIN CANDY |

IN THE FIRST YEAR OF LIFE, A BABY'S BRAIN TRIPLES IN WEIGHT.

AT AGE 3, A BABY'S BRAIN IS TWICE AS ACTIVE AS AN ADULT'S.

EVERY YEAR 200 MILLION CHILDREN UNDER THE AGE OF 5 FAIL TO REACH THEIR FULL SOCIAL AND COGNITIVE POTENTIAL.

GO TO PAGE 178 FOR MORE TIPS AND INFORMATION
Source: The Dana Guide for Brain Health, World Health Organization.

EVENING
Fam Jam
8:45 p.m.

Bully *Alert*

Stand Up, Speak Out

IF TWO TEENS CAN STOP A BULLY with not much more than the colour pink, think what else we can accomplish by speaking out. David Shepherd and Travis Price, two senior students at Central Kings High School in the small town of Cambridge, Nova Scotia, heard that bullies were harassing a freshman for wearing a pink shirt to class. They realized that staying silent meant condoning bullying – something Travis experienced first-hand when he was younger. The two quickly pulled together a plan and shared it with friends via Facebook, Instant Messenger and good old-fashioned word of mouth. The next day the freshman and the bullies were shocked to see a sea of pink: 700 students all wearing pink T-shirts in solidarity. The good news story spread through major news networks and even onto the *Ellen DeGeneres Show*. Today, the wave of pink sweeps the nation as schools across Canada and abroad celebrate the anti-bullying Pink Shirt Day in February and September – a little reminder of what some colour (and courage) can do.

Bullying is not just a high school phenomenon. In the adult world, bullying persists in boardrooms, bars, on the bus and Internet. We see it in the news when a poor nation is forced to accept an unfair trade deal or a dictator uses violence on peaceful protesters. Problems that have grown so huge started somewhere small. What if in the beginning one person had said, "This is not right"? At the time, your comment might seem insignificant. But each time you speak out it gets a little easier and spreads a feeling of tolerance and respect, something we can all appreciate. And, who knows, you might just inspire a movement, as David and Travis did.

TAKE NOTE

- Refuse to laugh with a bully. Even by cracking a smile when someone else is ridiculed means you approve. Make it clear that you don't.

- Enlist the help of an adult. If a child approaches you, worried about payback from a bully, brainstorm ways to defuse the situation quietly.

- When reporting a bullying incident, relate specific details of what happened. For instance, who pushed whom and exactly what was said.

- Make friends with a victim of bullying. Bullies often pick on someone perceived as having weak ties with the group. Parents: encourage your child to keep up strong friendships to guard against bullies.

- Cyber-bullying through social networks and cell phones can be just as powerful as face-to-face harassment. Keep the home computer in a central place and make it clear that your child should not make hurtful comments or tease anyone online. Also, watch out for warning signs such as getting upset at the computer, blocking the screen from view or a reluctance to attend school.

SOLID TIP

BULLYING HURTS | *Bullying has serious effects on the playground and beyond.*

FAST AND FURIOUS
Bullying occurs once every seven minutes on the playground and lasts approximately 38 seconds.

CLOSE TO SCHOOL
Incidents happen within 120 feet of school 68% of the time.

THE BULLY EFFECT
90% of those bullied experience a drop in grades, increased anxiety and a loss of friends or a social life.

GO TO PAGE 178 FOR MORE TIPS AND INFORMATION
Source: University of Alberta and Queen's University.

RAISING SOCIALLY CONSCIOUS KIDS

Michaëlle Jean

Canada's former Governor General Michaëlle Jean has waged a life-long battle against indifference. She escaped a dictatorship in Haiti to become a top broadcaster in her adopted country of Canada. Today, she works as UNESCO's Special Envoy to Haiti, while running a creative arts foundation for disadvantaged youth. As she raises her daughter Marie Eden to confront the challenges of the modern world, she tries to set an example of compassion every day.

THE MOMENT: "I was raised in Haiti under the Duvalier dictatorship in a country with many, many challenges. But I was raised by parents who fought illiteracy, and for civil rights and justice and they paid a high price for that. My father was arrested and tortured; my whole family was forced to come to Canada. But, as parents, they set a rule that we could never, never be indifferent. For a child, that's difficult, but I think children need to be aware."

THE MISSION: "I think Marie Eden has learned that from her parents for sure. She's seen me in action for five years as Governor General. She's also the daughter of a filmmaker, my husband, Jean-Daniel Lafond, who explores many difficult perspectives in his work. She's seen as a mediator at her school already, because she hates to see children being intimidated or bullied. Instead of running away from it, she knows she has the responsibility to do something."

THE HABIT: "After the earthquake in Haiti, Marie Eden saw the generous response coming from across the country. Everyone cared; no one was indifferent. She began making bracelets to fundraise and she told me, 'We want to twin our school with a school in Haiti, because we have a lot to learn from the children there, as much as we have to give.' That spirit of reciprocity is clear in her mind. But, you know, she's not unique. I see this in children across Canada."

MICHAËLLE JEAN TRIES TO SET AN EXAMPLE FOR HER DAUGHTER

> " *Sometimes, the people who impress you the most are not people of power, kings or heads of state. Sometimes they are 11 years old.* "

Evening
AFTER
HOURS

9:00 a.m.
10:00 a.m.
11:00 a.m.
12:00 p.m.
1:00 p.m.
2:00 p.m.
3:00 p.m.
4:00 p.m.
5:00 p.m.
6:00 p.m.
7:00 p.m.
8:00 p.m.
9:00 p.m.
10:00 p.m.
11:00 p.m.
12:00
1:0
a.m
:00 a.m.
4:00 a.m.
5:00 a.m.
6:00 a.m.
7:00 a.m.

Pet *Rescue*

Be an Animal's Superhero

MEET TUNA. Don't be fooled by the name: she's actually an 8 year old cat, rescued from the streets of Vancouver's downtown east side. Meghan McKiernan, a 30 year old grant writer, took one look at the scrawny grey feline with two missing toes and adopted her on the spot. At first, Tuna hid all day, only coming out at night to eat (not necessarily tuna!) and to visit the litter box. The cat was terrified of men – a problem for Meghan's live-in boyfriend, who began to feel like Shrek each time he entered a room and the cat whimpered. Concerned, Meghan read the cat's records from the shelter: severe anxiety, fear of new people. Tuna had been this way forever. Meghan burst into tears. But the records noted that, given time, Tuna tended to warm up, so Meghan persevered.

Every year approximately 55,000 animals are euthanized, around half of all those surrendered to shelters. Puppy mills churn out animals in sickly conditions, while owners let pets wander around unspayed or unneutered. All this contributes to overpopulation and ultimately the destruction of many healthy animals. Growing up, we always had dogs (all weirdly named after food: Pepper, Coco, Brandy and Muffin) and we remember the hesitation around adopting a rescued animal that could have emotional problems. However, shelters today often provide owners with comprehensive behavior records and, as a last resort, an animal can be surrendered if a serious problem arises.

Three weeks after adopting, Meghan held Tuna for the first time. From there, the pair grew into perfect companions. Today, Tuna's sweetly attached to her owner, waking her every morning and meowing each night for her to come to bed. Before buying a brand new pet from a store or breeder, check your local shelter first. It's cheaper, guarantees your new pet is fixed, and provides a home for a pet that truly needs it. For Meghan, knowing Tuna's struggles helped her bond with the cat. It turned out to be a happy ending for everyone: Tuna even warmed up to Meghan's boyfriend.

PHOTOGRAPHY BY RYAN BOLTON

BECOME A PET PAL

SOLID TIP

- Not ready for a long-term commitment? On a short-term basis try taking in animals that struggle in the shelter environment.

- When pet-hunting, ask friends and family if they know of an available animal, or scour Craigslist and other online classifieds for animal adoptions.

- Before taking an animal into your home, ensure that you have basic caring tools: litter box, leash, scratching post, any grooming equipment.

- Get your cat or dog neutered or spayed pronto, otherwise you'll have mini Spots or Fluffies running around before you know it.

- Ask before you buy at the local pet store, to make sure animals come from shelters or humane breeders rather than squalid puppy or kitty mills.

- Animals can help decrease stress in work places, hospitals, daycares or recovery centres. Ask around at organizations if you can donate a few hours of your good-natured pet's time to help relieve tension in stressful environments.

POWERFUL PET THERAPY

Soldiers suffering from post-traumatic stress disorder say having a dog overwhelmingly reduces symptoms and the use of meds.

Pets, like Hank here, not only reduce stress but also help keep us fit.

Studies show we have lower blood pressure when we're with our pets.

GO TO PAGE 179 FOR MORE TIPS AND INFORMATION
Source: Psychiatric Service Dog Society and University of Maryland.

Garden *Variety*

Share your Space

IT WAS SUMMERTIME and the trees were sprouting leaves, the soil bursting with flowers, but Kamal Mattar's backyard looked a little sad. As a surgeon who works in Niagara Falls, Kamal spends most of his time away from his Toronto house. After weeks of neglect, the backyard weeds had cleared the 15-foot fence; the soil looked sandy and grey. Kamal almost admitted defeat by calling in a SWAT team of landscapers but, instead, he found a website called SharingBackyards.com. It pairs too busy backyard-owners with green thumbs desperate for green space. This is how he met Laura Hamilton, an apartment-dweller who lived nearby. When we stopped by Kamal's backyard a month after they connected, Laura was happily watering raspberries, staking tomato bushes and pruning zucchini flowers – a bounty that Kamal is happy to leave to Laura.

Gardening ain't just grandma's turf anymore: it's a cheap, easy way to grow local, organic food. There are other bonuses, too: plants help soak up smog-causing particles, while gardening builds skills and community ties. Studies even show that a well-tended garden helps decrease vandalism and crime. In fact, gardening is so popular it rivals our country's love of hockey: 11 percent of Canadians over the age of 30 garden and only 5 percent of adult Canadians regularly play hockey. The only obstacle is that 40 percent of us go without our own little of bit Eden. Backyard shares between Kamal and Laura can help solve this disparity. If a perfect match isn't made online, hundreds of community gardens are in bloom outside high-rises, in parks or playgrounds.

Back in their shared garden, Laura plucked tomatoes that she would take home to transform into a winter's worth of pasta sauce, while work-weary Kamal strolled through a beautifully tended garden and admired the watermelons he suggested planting. As we watched the pair chat, we realized that this garden was growing not only fruits and veggies, but community as well.

SOLID TIP

ALL THE LEAFY THINGS

- Use organic approaches to controlling pests, such as ladybugs that eat up plant-eating insects or saucers of beer to drown slugs.

- Keep a lid on weeds by pulling them out before they seed.

- Let a bottle of Coke go flat and use it to kill off pesky weeds.

- Choose indigenous or native shrubs and flowers that require less water and pest control.

- Check out programs like Plant-a-Row, Grow-a-Row that collect your bumper crop of cucumbers and donate the fresh veggies to nutritionally starved food banks.

- Close to a third of our trash is food scraps – A.K.A. fertilizer-in-waiting – that seep nutrients into your soil. Not all municipalities have embraced the composting program yet, so create your own composter with a bin from the hardware store.

- Choose a person-powered lawn mower over a gasoline-fueled one. It's good exercise and produces no pollution.

TURF TIPS | *Create a real, live FarmVille!*

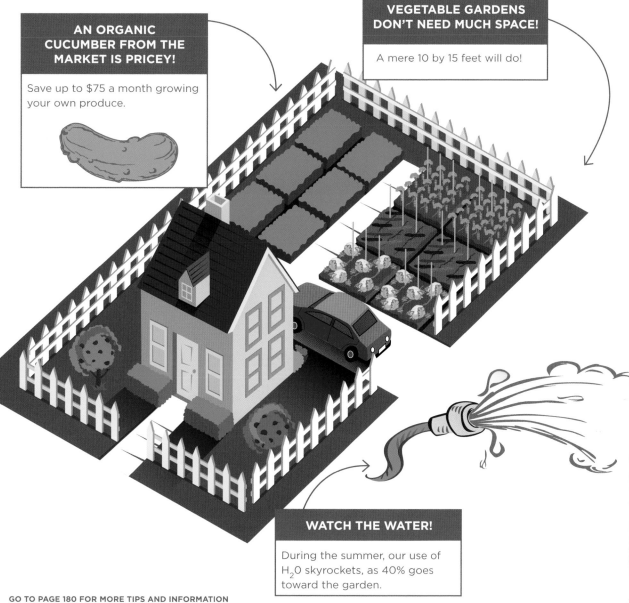

AN ORGANIC CUCUMBER FROM THE MARKET IS PRICEY!

Save up to $75 a month growing your own produce.

VEGETABLE GARDENS DON'T NEED MUCH SPACE!

A mere 10 by 15 feet will do!

WATCH THE WATER!

During the summer, our use of H_2O skyrockets, as 40% goes toward the garden.

GO TO PAGE 180 FOR MORE TIPS AND INFORMATION

Source: *New York Times*, *David Suzuki's Green Guide* (David Suzuki Foundation) and *The Green Book*.

The Gift that Keeps *Giving*

Give Socially Responsible Presents

LIKE ALL MOTHERS, Grace has high hopes for her five children. But this mama living in Kenya's Maasai Mara had all of her livestock — and her savings — wiped out by a drought. She could barely feed her family, let alone send her eldest son, John, to the paid high school anymore. Worst of all, she felt like she was letting her family down. Then Grace heard of a new business that paid women a fair wage for beading jewellery – a traditional practice in Maasai culture. Now Grace is part of the Me to We Artisans program (see right), where she spends what spare time she has hand-crafting bespoke bracelets, necklaces and belts. John is in school again. And back in Canada, savvy shoppers, celebrities and fashionistas that are wearing their heart on their sleeve are all wearing jewellery made by Grace and other mamas. They know it's not just any bling. That bracelet or friendship chain on their wrists and around their necks is moving Grace's story forward, helping her family take the next step in life.

Giving a gift shouldn't be a grind. Offer gifts that keep giving – to someone besides just the recipient. Today, with ethical and sustainable gifts, we can match a present to a passion, whether that's the environment, education or youth empowerment. There are entire companies devoted to sustainable shopping. TOMS, for example, gives a pair of shoes to a child in a developing country for every pair sold in North America. Or you can look for certain products in a larger brand line that donate profits to charity, such as the Charity Pot Lotion from Lush that gives money to grassroots charities around the world. While browsing, check whether a company pays its workers fair wages, minimizes its impact on the earth, and helps someone like Grace pursue her dreams.

GOOD TIDINGS

- Choose a theme for your gifts, such as supporting local businesses, expanding youth education in developing countries or protecting endangered species.

- Find out what issues matter to your friends and family and pick a gift that helps the cause.

- Donate livestock to a family in need or save an endangered species close to your heart.

- Give someone a card with vegetable or tree seeds so they can grow a gift that keeps on growing.

- Give the kids an experience they'll remember forever: go on a family volunteer trip and help out at an animal sanctuary or school in a developing country.

- Inquire at the store whether a certain product or line has any do-gooding initiatives, such as Bono's (RED) brand collaboration with such big-name corporations as Starbucks, GAP and Dell.

....| PRESENT & ACCOUNTED FOR|

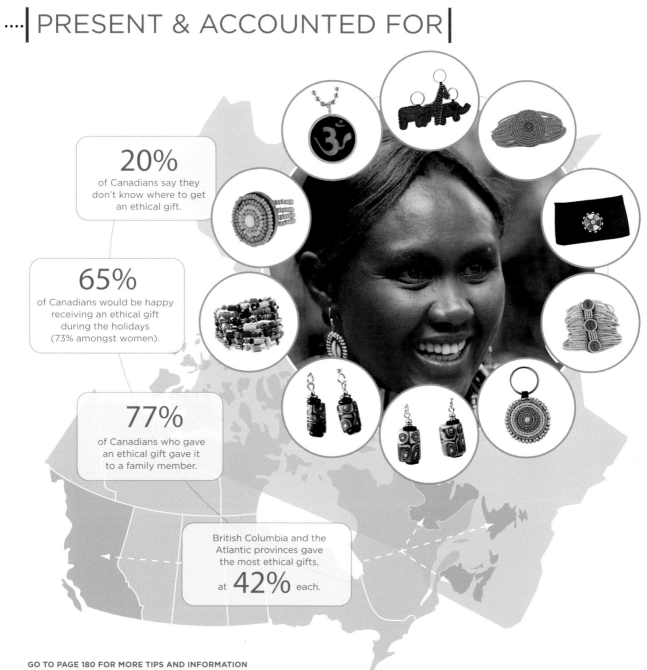

20%
of Canadians say they don't know where to get an ethical gift.

65%
of Canadians would be happy receiving an ethical gift during the holidays (73% amongst women).

77%
of Canadians who gave an ethical gift gave it to a family member.

British Columbia and the Atlantic provinces gave the most ethical gifts, at **42%** each.

GO TO PAGE 180 FOR MORE TIPS AND INFORMATION
Source: Plan Canada Ethical Gift Giving Survey.

Feel-Good Gifts

Give From the Heart

THE HOLIDAY SEASON generates stress almost as certain as death and taxes. But after years of impersonal gifts and stretched-thin budgets, Sunshine Wilson – a 37 year old mother of three from Ottawa – and her family called the gift-buying craze off. Her mom and dad, six siblings, their spouses and kids decided instead to make their gifts. One Christmas, they pulled names out of a hat, leaving a year to craft one special gift for someone else. Ten years later, the tradition has inspired some truly extraordinary presents that cost little to make. Her father, who quarries stone as a mason, constructed a Japanese garden. Sunshine repurposed the curtains of childhood bedrooms into a massive quilt. Her husband drew a portrait of their kids. A hammock was woven for the easygoing brother, a weekly dessert was baked for the dad with a sweet tooth, and a fleece picker was tooled for the mom, a weaver. They've all come to know and appreciate one another's tastes and abilities better than ever. Every year, when the big reveal draws near, that same holiday spirit builds – without all the killer credit card bills.

Instead of trolling the malls for presents, the best gifts come packed with meaning that money can't buy. Since Craig travels 300 days out of every year with nothing more than a backpack of essentials, we can't give him lots of stuff. In fact, the demands of building a social enterprise that involves the whole family means we've all become incredibly busy. This means the best gift we can give one another is time. We splurge on experiences instead, such as a ticket to a beloved band or a lavish homemade meal. We like to think that we're giving memories with mileage. Despite Craig's limited baggage space, he still drags trinkets and mementos back – perfect for someone back home. In this way, each gift reminds us that no matter how far he's travelled, he's thinking of us.

GET CRAFTY

- If you're strapped for time, make part of your gift such as the card, wrapping paper or ribbons.

- Go old school with traditional decorations like strung-together popcorn and cranberries or gingerbread cookie ornaments.

- Try sourcing all your gifts from one place, such as a craft fair or local artisan you admire, to support nearby businesses and buy handmade in one go.

- Something old becomes new again. Scour flea markets, vintage stores, antique shops and other purveyors of second-hand gear.

- Make an I.O.U. coupon book filled with friendly gestures loved ones can claim, such as cupcakes or a road trip adventure.

- Do away with the re-gift stigma: if you have something great and useful collecting dust in the basement, give it to someone else.

- Give a beloved photo of yours and turn it into a special gift by framing it yourself.

- Whip up a batch of cookies or candies and package them in pretty containers.

SOLID TIP

···· | WASTE NOT, WANT NOT |

Every year, we churn through a massive amount of waste and cash at holiday time.

More than **two billion** cards are thrown away.

40% of batteries are bought at this time.

Over **$4 billion** is spent on wrapping paper, decorations and gifts.

GO TO PAGE 181 FOR MORE TIPS AND INFORMATION
Source: Recycling Council of B.C., Lunenberg Community Recycling Centre.

The Movie is the *Message*

Get Entertained ... And Informed

WHEN A TYPICAL 48 HOURS includes a red eye from Toronto to Chicago and another to India, you can imagine that a lot of our entertainment comes in the form of cheesy in-flight movies. Catch us back on earth relaxing in a theatre and we often opt for brainless films with our popcorn and soda. We like our high-speed car chases. We love our exploding buildings. And somehow it became ingrained in us that hard-hitting commentary or real-world issues do not quicken the pulse.

But our preconception that education and entertainment can't mix was due for a reset. After seeing movies such as *Syriana* and *Charlie Wilson's War*, we were riveted. Montreal-born Jeff Skoll, founder of Participant Media and producer of these two flicks, including the landmark global warming documentary *An Inconvenient Truth*, managed to convince two armchair action heroes like us that entertainment could carry a message. Travelling with us in Kenya, Skoll explained his mission to marry fast-paced action with information. The aim, of course, is to get bums in the seats. But he also wants to relay a message, maybe even spark a movement. Watching other great films, such as Ed Burtynsky's *Manufactured Landscapes* and Yung Chang's *Up the Yangtze*, both Canadian docs, mean we don't have to sacrifice our love for drama in place of a meaningful message. They go hand in hand. We look to CBC's jazzed-up new radio shows, such as Jian Ghomeshi's *Q*, or TV shows like *George Stroumboulopoulos Tonight*. With all the colourful options out there, the divide between information and entertainment is no longer black and white.

SOLID TIP

OUR FAVOURITE BLOGS, MAGAZINES, APPS, TV SHOWS AND PEOPLE:

- *Huffington Post*: celebrity tabloid pieces are mixed with hard-hitting commentary and coverage reports on political events.

- *The Onion*: fake news articles succinctly point major world problems while splitting your sides with guffaws.

- *Rick Mercer Report*: CBC's national treasure, Rick Mercer, does amazingly even-handed rants on topics political as well as mundane.

- *This Hour Has 22 Minutes*: another favourite for satirical, Canada-focused commentary.

- *Colbert Report, Jon Stewart*: These guys interview some of the most cutting-edge thinkers and shakers and pick up on some of the most socially relevant issues of the time.

- NFB Films App: Canada's publicly funded film organization offers 10,000 movies, on a range of international and Canadian issues, for free on your smartphone.

- Global TV's *Currents*: Check out the major news networks' hard-hitting series on issues ranging from brothels to foreign nannies.

- Kevin Newman: The former Global National anchor is now producing insightful and highly watchable documentaries such as *No Country for Animals* (on animal rights in Canada) and *Missing the Target* (on gun control).

MEDIA THAT MOVES YOU

Me to We specializes in providing television, books, movies and music. Check out some of our current favourites below!

LESSONS FROM A STREET KID

A beautifully illustrated children's book with an important life lesson for socially conscious kids.

DEGRASSI GOES TO KENYA DVD

The teen cast of the popular CTV show *Degrassi* travelled to Kenya to build a much-needed school and a documentary crew tagged along to capture their transformational journey.

MY MAASAI LIFE

From the suburbs of Illinois to the dusty Maasai Mara region of Kenya, this compelling autobiographical book charts the voyage of one intrepid and inspirational woman. Great for educators, families and young adults.

STANDING TALL

Read the inspiring story of Spencer West, who never let physical challenges stand in his way. Ever.

GO TO PAGE 182 FOR MORE TIPS AND INFORMATION

PUPPY LOVE

George
Stroumboulopoulos

Every night on CBC, George Stroumboulopoulos bounds across the stage of *George Stroumboulopoulos Tonight*, greeting politicians, hockey players and musicians alike with boundless energy. But this animal lover could just as easily be hanging out in a dog park. In the past, Strombo worked with rescued pit bulls and he still loves getting down with pups from rough-and-tumble backgrounds whenever he gets the chance.

THE MOMENT: "In the past, I used to foster dogs and help out with foster animals. I remember after a long day of doing a show, I'd come home, crawl into bed, put the TV on and just mellow. All of a sudden, Dre (I name all the dogs after musicians) would jump up on the bed and put his head on my chest and fall asleep. It was a very calm, peaceful moment. I miss those moments with those dogs. In the end, when we found the dog a good home, I was very happy for the dog, but it was really hard to say good-bye. But, I had a couple dogs and the girl I was dating had a couple, so there were a lot of dogs in our life."

THE HABIT: "Basically, you take a dog that was in a compromised position and foster it back to health, socialize it and find it a home. I found that with the pit bulls I rescued – dogs that were generally in bad situations beforehand – when they finally begin to trust and love you, do they ever open up! I want an animal with a life and a story and its own character."

PHOTOGRAPHY BY JOSH SAM

GEORGE BACKSTAGE ON THE SET OF HIS TELEVISION SHOW.

66 *At one point, I had four pit bulls and nine snakes in my basement apartment. I was practically Steve Irwin."*

RESOURC GUIDE

WELCOME TO A COMPENDIUM OF LIVING ME TO WE RESOURCES. Here, you'll find books to read, websites to scroll, acts to make, products to purchase and more recommendations on socially conscious living. Check out the READ-WATCH-LISTEN headings for books, movies, websites, podcasts and more, ACT for things you can do right now and BUY to find products that will improve your impact on the earth and community. Visit the online Living Me to We forum at www.metowe.com to share your own resources and recommendations with other socially conscious Canadians. Live the change!

JAVA JOLT

READ • LISTEN • WATCH

BLACK GOLD
blackgoldmovie.com
Watch this award-winning documentary on the injustices of the coffee trade and its effect on poor countries around the world.

BBC'S *THE COST OF COFFEE* PODCAST
news.bbc.co.uk/2/hi/programmes/documentary_archive/6609141.stm
Listen along as the BBC tracks the journey of a cup of coffee from the farm to the supermarket to the cup, with the price escalating 16 times along the way. Surprise ending: very little of that cash gets to the farmer.

ACT

SUPPORT LOCAL
Find an independently owned café in your 'hood where you can get to know the locals and linger over a cup of joe.

BOIL WHAT YOU NEED
Filling the kettle to the max seems like a good idea, but if you only need one cup you end up releasing unnecessary CO_2 into the air.

TALK WITH SELLERS
The more you get to know your local coffee purveyors, you'll feel more comfortable asking questions about where they get their coffee beans.

BUY

BULK BEANS, LOOSE LEAF
Cut down on packaging by purchasing tea and coffee in bulk.

TEA BALL, REUSABLE FILTERS
Rather than running your morning pick-me-up through a disposable, bleached coffee filter or throwing away tea bags regularly, purchase a cheap gold filter for your coffee machine or a tea ball.

SAVE WATER

READ • LISTEN • WATCH

CBC'S *WATER: INDEPTH*
cbc.ca/news/background/water
In a series of CBC articles and radio shows, the national broadcaster took one comprehensive look at global water issues, all filtered through a Canadian lens.

WATERLIFE
Narrated by Gord Downie of The Tragically Hip, this documentary surveys the state of one of Canada's great water resources, now threatened by chemical contaminates, invasive species and climate change.

THE STORY OF BOTTLED WATER
storyofstuff.org
Part of a series of popular online videos by activist Annie Leonard, this one picks apart the massively wasteful production of bottled water.

BLUE GOLD: WORLD WATER WARS
bluegold-worldwaterwars.com
A scary documentary on the coming implications of privatized and commoditized water.

ACT

SHOW ME THE GREEN
showmethegreen.ca
Make an environmental upgrade on your house using this amazingly comprehensive search engine that pulls up government grants and rebates to help with the cost.

WORLD WATER DAY
unwater.org/worldwaterday
Take part in the UN global awareness day on March 22 by starting a water-focused event or campaign in your area.

TO TUB OR TO SHOWER
If you're looking to just get clean, keep the shower to a speedy 5-minute rinse. Opting for a bath? Plug it before you run it.

SHAVING OFF TIME
Shaving your legs over the sink, rather than in the shower, can shave minutes off your usual running water time. Some flexibility is required.

BUY

LOW FLOW SHOWERHEAD
gaiam.com
Check out these water conserving showerheads that reduce the amount of water with no noticeable difference in pressure. Some also come with quick shut-off switches for scrubbing-up time.

FOLDABLE WATER BOTTLE
vapur.us/anti-bottle

You will never again have a reason to buy a bottle of water with these handy water holders that fold into tiny little squares of light-weight, BPA-free plastic. Also, they're freezable, easy to wash and come with a handy carabiner to hang off your bag or knapsack.

CLOTHES MINDED

READ • WATCH • LISTEN

THE TRAVELS OF A T-SHIRT IN THE GLOBAL ECONOMY
An economist and business prof takes on finding out where clothing comes from and where it goes after we're done with it.

WORN MAGAZINE
While the focus of this quarterly magazine is not necessarily sustainable clothing, the mag has extra special love for vintage (read: recycled) clothing.

DEADLY NIGHTSHADES
nightshadesbikecrew.blogspot.com

This bike gang and design collective makes ethical and sustainable clothing design super cool. Plus, they have great blog that explores these topics in a fun, interesting and cool way.

ACT

SPREAD THE WORD
Found an ethical brand you love? Tell people about it, through word of mouth, blogs and social media networking sites.

BUY

ME TO WE STYLE
metowestyle.com

The clothing arm of Me to We applies its principles to fashion: for each t-shirt sold, a tree is planted, everything is produced fairly and in Canada using organic cotton and bamboo fabrics.

PATAGONIA
patagonia.com

A California-based sportswear company that kicks serious butt when it comes to eco-friendly, ethically produced clothing.

ICEBREAKER
icebreaker.com

A Kiwi company that specializes in active-wear clothing made from sustainable wool, and focuses on making its entire production cycle transparent and fair.

OLIBERTE SHOES
oliberte.com

Committed to fair-trade and building a strong economy in Africa, these shoes are manufactured there and sold in Canada.

MODROBES
modrobes.com

This brand has morphed from putting out those billowy pants held up with a buckle into a slick and ethical sportswear clothing company.

ETHICAL OCEAN
ethicalocean.com

Seamlessly links ethical products (including clothing) with ethical shoppers and ships right to your door.

CHEMICALS IN COSMETICS

READ • WATCH • LISTEN

NO MORE DIRTY LOOKS: THE TRUTH ABOUT YOUR BEAUTY PRODUCTS
nomoredirtylooks.com

A great guide to the chemical perpetrators in cosmetics, along with brand recommendations and make-your-own beauty recipes.

THE GREEN BEAUTY GUIDE
juliegabriel.com

Another helpful guide to natural beauty alternatives, along with shopping lists and multi-purpose recipes for an avocado facial as well as an avocado Rueben sandwich.

SKIN DEEP
cosmeticsdatabase.com

Dare to find out what's in your favourite lipstick by searching this comprehensive database of over 60,000 products, complete with ratings and explanations of all those tricky 10-syllable ingredient names.

DAVID SUZUKI'S DIRTY DOZEN GUIDE
davidsuzuki.org/publications/downloads/2010/whats-inside-shoppers-guide.pdf

Download this wallet-size guide and you'll never forget what sodium laureth sulfate or PEG means when you're in the market for some safe cosmetics.

QUEEN OF GREEN
davidsuzuki.org

This blog, run by Lindsay Coulter of the David Suzuki Foundation, covers a range of green living topics and offers many home beauty recipes as well.

ACT

FEMME TOXIC
femmetoxic.com
This Montreal girls' group is running events and raising awareness about the hazardous chemicals in cosmetics. Start your own chapter!

CAMPAIGN FOR SAFE COSMETICS
safecosmetics.org
This lobbying group, started by the Breast Cancer Fund in 2004, has run a number of successful campaigns and suggests a range of volunteer options, from tabling at a local event to hosting a safe home-brewing cosmetics party.

MAKE YOUR OWN
Try your hand at brewing up your cosmetics using the books and websites above.

BUY

WELL.CA
well.ca
This Guelph, Ontario-based company ships free to anywhere in Canada and offers competitive prices on organic, vegan and Canadian-made products.

DR. HAUSCHKA
drhauschka.com
This cutting-edge company uses ingredients straight from its own garden to make concealers out of carrot extract and lipstick out of seed butter.

DRUIDE
druide.ca
Quebec's affordable Druide line sells a full range of products all certified by the third-party, independent label EcoCert.

LIVE CLEAN
live-clean.com
These products steer clear of nasty chemicals and are sold in Shoppers Drug Mart and other mainstream stores.

ROCKY MOUNTAIN SOAP COMPANY
rockymountainsoap.com
The aptly named west-coast Rocky Mountain Soap Company sells completely natural products.

WHOLE FOODS
This natural food company is rapidly expanding its selection of cosmetics and personal care products.

CLOTHING REPAIR

READ • LISTEN • WATCH

THE STORY OF STUFF
storyofstuff.org
If you ever needed proof that we buy too much stuff, just check out this popular online video series that clearly outlines the world's wasteful approach to bottled water, cosmetics, electronics and more.

SEWING BLOGS
sewcraftful.com
craftster.org
There are hundreds of design and sewing craft blogs out on the Internet, chockfull of designs and patterns to make at home. Check out Sew Craftful that includes links to free sewing books, or Craftster with its many sewing pattern challenges.

ACT

SEWING SPACE
Start your own sewing, knitting or crafting night at your house by inviting a few enterprising friends and spreading the word.

GET INSPIRED
Check out etsy.com and other design blogs for some great homemade projects you can try out yourself.

WASH INSIDE OUT
Turn your jeans and shirts inside out when machine washing and drying. This will preserve the colours and keep your clothes looking fresh longer.

AIR DRY
Install a clothing line to air dry your clothing during the warmer months. This conserves energy, extends the life of your clothing and leaves them smelling like sunlight.

BUY

SEWING KIT
Purchase a cheap kit of multi-coloured spools of thread, mini scissors and needles for quick repairs on the go.

SEWING MACHINE
For the really gung-ho, invest in a sewing machine to handle more major clothing repairs.

KNITTING NEEDLES AND YARN
Idle hands no more! Take up

knitting and you'll be able to darn your socks and make warm-weather gear yourself.

FUN FABRIC

Search out fabric shops with funky patterns and get inspired about what you could create.

EAT LESS MEAT

READ • LISTEN • WATCH

THE MEATRIX
themeatrix.com

This interactive series of webisodes and video games frames the social, environmental and moral problems of factory farming system in a Matrix-themed plot line (meet Moopheus and Leo the pig).

FAST FOOD NATION

The best-selling book by investigative journalist Eric Schlosser exposes the seamy underbelly of the mainstream food system.

FOOD INC.

Covering all aspects and indiscretions of the global food system, this film will make you want to know where your food, particularly your meat, comes from.

HEALTHY OCEAN BLOG
davidsuzuki.org/blogs/healthy-oceans-blog

The David Suzuki Foundation's blog provides sustainable seafood suggestions and covers issues related to the fish stock and water systems in Canada.

HEALTHY OCEAN BOOK

Even if you're not ready to take the vegan plunge, this book has tons of handy tips and suggestions for a reduced meat intake. *Arsenal Pulp Press: 1999.*

ACT

PREP VEGGIES

Wash and cut up vegetables a few days before using – this makes it much more likely that you will snack on them or use in meals. Word of warning: cut-up produce moulders faster so use these up quickly.

MEATLESS MONDAYS
meatlessmonday.com Join this online movement that challenges people, one day a week, to go meatless. The website is chock full of recipes and meat alternatives.

BUY

MEATLESS PROTEIN

Try tofu, tempeh (a denser soy bean cake) and a variety of beans for a perfect protein punch.

A VEGETARIAN COOKBOOK

Look to veggie or vegan cookbooks for inspiration, preferably one with lots of tantalizing photos to get your taste buds excited.

GET INFORMED

READ • LISTEN • WATCH

INNOVATION CANADA
innovationcanada.ca

An online magazine that covers new and interesting research from Canadian universities and think-tanks.

TED TALKS
ted.com

This informal lecture series feature prominent thinkers tackling the biggest obstacles of the day. You can download as a podcast or watch online.

WE DAY U
weday.com

Watch the inspirational speakers of We Day from Deepak Chopra to the Dalai Lama, talk about changing the world.

ITUNES U

This easy-to-use lecture collection is free on the iTunes store. You can take a course in marketing or listen to a Yale professor expound on evolution.

HUFFINGTON POST CANADA
huffingtonpost.ca

The popular American blog now has a Canadian counterpart that comes with a special environmentally focused section.

HOW STUFF WORKS
howstuffworks.com

Basically a reliable-version of Wikipedia, this Discovery Company website breaks down the nuts and bolts of history, science, art and pretty much any topic you ever wanted to know in blog, podcast or article form. Check out the Stuff You Should Know podcast that explores one topic (Vikings, molecular gastronomy, microcredit and more!) in 30-minute segments.

ACT

TWITTER
twitter.com
Signing up doesn't mean you have to tweet constantly, but an account allows access to all the up-to-the-minute coverage of breaking news stories.

BECOME A CITIZEN JOURNALIST
Arm yourself with a camera and document local news stories that you deem important.

SUPPORT INDEPENDENT MEDIA
Attend small magazine launches or click on ads of the small blogs you like – this all helps support the small media you love.

BUY

AUDIBLE.COM
audible.com
Download the daily *New York Times*, or whatever new hit book is on shelves, direct to your smartphone.

SUBSCRIBE
Government subsidies make Canadian magazines much cheaper than their American counterparts, so why not get a subscription? For a listing of all the great Canadian publications out there, check out Magazines Canada.

eREADER
For media fiends, iPads and other electronic readers can make access to news even easier and trim the paper reliance.

VAMPIRE POWER

READ • LISTEN • WATCH

TREEHUGGER.COM
This popular blog from the Discovery Company covers environmental news with many regular updates on sustainable improvements for your home.

CANADA MORTGAGE AND HOUSING CORPORATION
www.cmhc-schl.gc.ca
This government-owned corporation offers tons of information on home improvement and sustainable building standards.

PLANETFORWARD
www.planetforward.ca
This sustainable shopping site also runs an informative blog called The Sustainable Scribe that details all sorts of helpful green home tips.

ACT

KEEP THE DOOR CLOSED
Quit the lolly-gagging in front of the fridge — it's one of the biggest energy hogs in the house.

CLEAN THE LINT BASKET
Keeping up on your lint cleaning duties will help your dryer operate at its best capacity, as will running a full load.

HIT THE OFF BUTTON
Avoid leaving your computer running.

BUY

ENERGY STAR APPLIANCES
This government-approved label tells you that an appliance uses 10 to 65 percent less energy and water, depending on the product.

BULLFROG POWER
bullfrogpower.com
Opt for green, renewable power from wind and hydro facilities that have been deemed low impact by Environment Canada and the EcoLogo label.

MOTION SENSOR LIGHTS
Get Energy Star-approved motion sensor lights for your home and garden, so energy is used only when needed.

TELECOMMUTE

READ • LISTEN • WATCH

CANADA TELEWORK ASSOCIATION
ivc.ca
This non-profit organization keeps a website on the goings-on in the telework industry, including job postings, studies and success stories.

ACT

CHEAPER RATES LIST
Find out if your Internet service provider offers special rates for home office Internet.

ENVIRONMENTAL COSTS
Trim your telecommuting carbon footprint, watch your energy

use: turn off lights, adjust your thermostat, combine cords to one power outlet and double up car-dependent errands.

MAKE A ROUTINE

and stick to it! Set aside certain hours of your day for email, phone calls and focus time.

KEEP IN TOUCH

Schedule a coffee with co-workers after office hours or on the weekend.

USE ONLINE TOOLS

Try free and shareable online calendars, docs and scheduling to keep on top of what you and your colleagues are working on.

TALK IT OUT

Meet with your supervisor to determine which days are best for you to work from home. You may want to bring up the at-home costs (such as printing, faxing, Internet) and insurance liabilities that may arise from working at home.

BUY

PASSWORD PROTECTORS, ANTI-VIRUS SOFTWARE, EXTERNAL HARD DRIVE

If you're going to be working on your home computer, you may want to consider added security and data protection for your computer.

NOISE CANCELLING HEADPHONES, EARPLUGS

No matter where you are, there are still distractions. Look into a pair of plugs to keep noisy attention-sucks at bay.

COMFORTABLE DESK CHAIR

Don't underestimate the power of office ergonomics! Having a comfortable chair can make a big improvement on your work habits.

OFFICE DÉCOR

Give your home office a few personal touches to truly turn it into a professional work space.

ALTERNATIVE TRANSPORTATION

READ • LISTEN • WATCH

ECOMOBILITY TV
ecomobility.tv
This great video and blog breaks down the issues on environmental choices for drivers, cyclists and pedestrians, for instance how to choose an eco-friendly car or the recyclability of your vehicle.

THE URBAN BIKING HANDBOOK: THE DIY GUIDE TO BUILDING, REBUILDING, TINKERING WITH, AND REPAIRING YOUR BICYCLE FOR CITY LIVING

A great beginner's guide, with information on the pros and cons of various bike types, bicycle lingo and repairs.

SUSTAINABLE CITIES COLLECTIVE
sustainablecitiescollective.com
This blog details everything to do with sustainable city growth, from smart growth to Richard Florida's latest piece on creative cities.

OTHER LAB
otherlab.com
This collective, which includes a software engineer, a mechanical engineer and a physicist, focuses on creating new and alternative forms of transportation. The blog is a fascinating mix of current transportation projects (check out the Onya Cycle – a front-loader bicycle!) and ideas for remaking how we get around.

JEFF SPECK
jeffspeck.com
Co-author of the influential book, *Suburban Nation: The Rise of Sprawl and the Decline of the American Dream*, keeps a Huffington Post blog about transportation and city-planning issues.

ACT

COMMUTER CHALLENGE
commuterchallenge.ca
Every year thousands of Canadians take part in the Commuter Challenge (June 5 to 11) as part of National Environment Week. Get your whole workplace in on the game of using nothing but sustainable transportation for one full week.

CARPOOL BULLETIN
commuterchallenge.ca
Set up an informal carpool network at your workplace or in the neighbourhood by posting "Ride Wanted" or "Riders Needed" posters nearby.

ROLLERBLADE, SKATEBOARD
Leave yourself some extra time in the morning and pick a fun way

to get to work instead.

WALK THIS WAY

Start a walking club with your colleagues, meeting up at various points along your route to work.

PLAN A CAR-FREE DAY

Start an annual car-free day at your work, brainstorming and facilitating ways to get to work without a vehicle.

CAR AUDIT

If your vehicle is of a certain age, run it through an emissions and maintenance check to make sure it's still running as clean as it can. Check your province or territory's transportation website to see if your car qualifies.

A CHANGE OF CLOTHING

Biking to work is all the more pleasant when you have clean clothes waiting for you.

CRITICAL MASS

Advocate for more bike lanes and the biking lifestyle every month, by riding en masse with a crew of cyclists, in most cities, on the last Friday of every month.

....
BUY
....

HELMET, REFLECTORS AND PORTABLE TOOL KIT

Before you get cycling, make sure to purchase all the accessories to get you there safely.

TRANSIT CARD

Try out public transit for a month by purchasing a pass in your city. You'll be surprised how much you use it, plus the feds offer tax rebates off your purchase.

PANNIER BAG
mec.ca

Nothing is more of a drag than being weighed down by heavy groceries. A bike bag can fix that. Mountain Equipment Co-op has a range of cheap, durable bags.

TRAIL MAPS

Search out a local biking – or walking – trail map for your city or town.

CAR SHARE MEMBERSHIP
carsharing.ca

If you occasionally need four wheels, consider getting a car sharing membership to cut down on rental or purchasing costs. This website features cross-country listings.

SCOOTER, E-BIKE

Individual vehicles like these that run on electric batteries or on small, fuel-efficient engines are on the rise in cities across Canada.

FUEL-EFFICIENT CARS
green-car-guide.com

Hybrid vehicles are already in the mainstream, while electric cars are on the way. If you're in the market for a new car, check out Natural Resources Canada's yearly testing of fuel-efficient vehicles.

COMMUTER ETIQUETTE

....
READ • LISTEN • WATCH
....

THE COMMUTER CHRONICLES
commuterchronicles.com

A hilarious collection of commuter experiences. This website will make you feel like

your commute is a breeze.

SEEN READING
bookmadam.squarespace.com/ seen-reading

This Toronto-run blog offers fictional, and often endearing, profiles of people seen reading on the subway and around town.

CULTURE SMART: A QUICK GUIDE TO CUSTOMS AND ETIQUETTE
kuperard.co.uk/culturesmart

Etiquette may seem a logical thing, but not so much when visiting a foreign country where everything from the rules of the road to table manners can be wildly different. This series publishes country guides available for anywhere from Russia to Egypt to Norway, each of which explain the finer points of a country's etiquette.

....
ACT
....

DISCUSSION TIME

Turn a long drive into a time to connect with your kids and partner. Encourage the family to put the gadgets away and instead share stories from the day.

BRING A BOOK

Plan ahead for a long commute with an engaging read to help pass the time pleasantly.

LIKE IT
facebook.com/group. php?gid=12518363366

Need to vent? Join this Facebook group on commuter etiquette.

BUY

ITUNES MUSIC ACCOUNT
Tune out loud music or overheard conversations by keeping a carefully curated selection of music for your way to work.

AUDIBLE.COM
This growing collection of read-aloud books includes thousands of classics as well as new releases.

ELECTRONIC WASTE

READ • LISTEN • WATCH

CRADLE TO CRADLE
This visionary book sets out a new and inspiring way of creating the products in our life, one where we don't reduce, reuse and recycle, but where old products source the new. Hence, cradle to cradle, rebirth to rebirth.

THE STORY OF ELECTRONICS
storyofstuff.org/electronics
The popular Story of Stuff videos have branched out to cover different wasteful issues, such as bottled water and, you guessed it, electronics.

RESOURCE RECYCLING
resource-recycling.com
An online magazine and newsletter featuring the latest news about recycling and composting, as well as issues related to the collection, handling and processing of scrap electronics.

GREENPEACE: GUIDE TO GREENER ELECTRONICS
greenpeace.org
This handy online guide ranks 18 of the top electronics manufacturers on a scale of one to 10.

ACT

GET THE WARRANTY
Whenever you can, purchase a warranty for your electronics to extend the life of your gadget and save on repair costs.

IREPAIR
irepair.ca
Before you toss that old iPod, check out this repair biz that works exclusively on Apple products and may be able to save your electronics when their warranties expire.

START A RECYCLING PROGRAM
In rural areas, recycling depots can sometimes be a drive away. Set up an informal drop-off program with your neighbours and friends, swapping drop-off duties and collection points.

GIVE IT AWAY
Check out the free section of Craigslist.com or Freecycle.org to find a home for your old, though still perfectly good, electronics.

PROTECT YOUR DATA
geepinc.com
Organizations such as GEEP recycle electronics responsibly and domestically, while protecting your data – particularly helpful for businesses.

BUY

RECYCLING BINS
Keep printer cartridges, batteries and old electronics separate with small, handy recycling bins.

RECHARGEABLE BATTERIES
When buying an electronic device, such as a camera, search out an option with a rechargeable battery.

SOLAR CHARGER
freeplayenergy.com
Rather than charging your gadgets off the grid, use solar or crank power battery. Check out the mobile chargers and flashlights here.

ME TO WE WORKPLACE

READ • LISTEN • WATCH

DON'T SWEAT THE SMALL STUFF AT WORK
dontsweat.com
This popular self-help series takes on one of the most commonly stressful parts of life and breaks it down in a hundred ways to ease stress and see the best in your workplace and co-workers.

ACT

SLOW DOWN AND SMILE
Even if you're in a rush, projecting an approachable, easygoing mien eases workplace tension. Plus, people will feel more comfortable reaching out to help or ask questions.

TEAM LUNCH
Commit to a regular lunch for the whole team once a week, whether

it's BYOL (bring-your-own-lunch), ordering in (pass around an order sheet to get everyone in on the action) or eating out for special occasions.

SHARE INSPIRATION

Make a special time during a meeting for sharing something inspirational.

BUY

CANDY

Keep a bowl of candy replenished daily on your desk.

OFFICE CAMERA

Keep a camera around to record special occasions for the team.

CSR 1.0 EMPLOYEE VOLUNTEERISM

READ • LISTEN • WATCH

LUNCH & LEARN

Prepare a video or photo presentation for your co-workers during lunchtime to get everyone fired up about pitching in. Or invite in a speaker to tell a inspiring story of getting involved.

FREE THE CHILDREN'S OFFICE KIT
freethechildren.com/office/office%20kit.pdf

Peruse Free The Children's handy office kit for more ideas on engaging team members and fostering a compassionate workplace.

ACT

ONLINE MESSAGE BOARDS
ning.com

Use free social networking sites to create an online community, forums and message boards for you and your like-minded colleagues. This keeps the conversation going after work hours round up.

USE YOUR NETWORK
linkedin.com

Install a widget or badge on your LinkedIn page to show your support for your cause and garner more support.

BUY

A MEAL

Cover the cost of a meal for a co-worker and get everyone talking about the issues he or she is passionate about.

A MOVIE

Rent or buy your favourite documentary on an issue you care about and host a movie night at your house one Friday eve for other passionate co-workers.

CSR 2.0 RESPONSIBLE WORK CULTURE

READ • LISTEN • WATCH

FORBES CSR BLOG
blogs.forbes.com/csr

Business magazine Forbes runs a regularly updated blog on the evolving world of corporate social responsibility.

CONFESSIONS OF A RADICAL INDUSTRIALIST: PROFITS, PEOPLE, PURPOSE - DOING BUSINESS BY RESPECTING THE EARTH
us.macmillan.com/confessionsofaradicalindustrialist

This book tells the tale of businessman Ray Anderson's mission to do business in an environmental and compassionate manner.

GOOD TO GREAT: WHY SOME COMPANIES MAKE THE LEAP AND OTHERS DON'T
jimcollins.com

This extensively researched and persuasive book from expert Jim Collins shows how to steer a company through leadership, discipline and passion.

ACT

EMPLOYEE CLUB

Start a club for employees looking to volunteer. You can complement this initiative by designating a special meeting spot, planning agenda topics and offering food and drink.

VOLUNTEER TRIP
metowe.com/trips/adult

Consider a volunteer trip for employees. Whether it's only for a weekend or a week, it takes the group outside the usual office setting and builds the teamwork mentality.

MENTOR LUNCH

Set up a tradition among staffers that has a long-time staff member taking a new employees out for lunch. This helps informally pass along the traditions and outlook of the company.

NEWSLETTER

Start a company newsletter of upcoming activities and events to keep employees informed on what's up around the office.

MATCH CONTRIBUTIONS

Match employees' contributions to a charity of their choice.

DONATE A DAY'S PAY

Set up a donation program for employees to automatically donate a day's pay to a charity of choice.

TIME OFF

Give employees time off work to volunteer.

BUY

TEAM T-SHIRTS

Make everyone feel part of the movement with special team gear, such as t-shirts or hats, to wear on group volunteer activities.

INSPIRING LITERATURE

Distribute copies of your favourite inspiring reads around the office. Some of our favourites include the titles above (*Confessions of a Radical Industrialist* and *Good to Great*) as well as Robert Putnam's influential *Bowling Alone*.

ETHICAL INVESTING

READ • LISTEN • WATCH

CORPORATE KNIGHTS
corporateknights.ca
This quarterly mag focuses on stories of "clean capitalism," keeping track of the changing world of corporate social responsibility.

SIO: THE SOCIAL INVESTMENT ORGANIZATION
socialinvestment.ca
This national, membership-based organization can link you to all ethical investors across Canada in one handy database.

INVESTING FOR CHANGE: PROFIT FROM RESPONSIBLE INVESTMENT
booksforunderstanding.org
This slim book is a great backgrounder on the history and foundational principles of socially responsible investments.

CORPWATCH
corpwatch.org
This site covers the destructive policies and practices of a range of different industries (transportation, media and entertainment, telecommunications) and also offers a handy step-by-step guide to researching your own investments.

ACT

PROFESSIONAL HELP

Seek out helpful and ethical advice through the SIO (see above) and set up an appointment with one of their ethical advisor members to discuss your values and options.

ASK QUESTIONS

Your like-minded friends and acquaintances can be a great starting point on your path to ethical investments. Ask around for socially minded local businesses to support in your 'hood.

KNOW THY BANK

Banks are tricky beasts, so you can't just walk into any ol' branch and expect investment advice. Search out these labeled, investment-side institutions as they'll have more expertise in ethical investments.

TD Canada Trust: TD Waterhouse, **tdwaterhouse.ca**

Canadian Imperial Bank of Commerce: CIBC Wood Gundy, **woodgundy.com**

Royal Bank of Canada: RBC Dominion Securities, **rbcds.com**

Bank of Montreal: BMO Nesbitt Burns **bmonesbittburns.com**

Bank of Nova Scotia: ScotiaMcLeod, **scotiabank.com**

National Bank Financial **nbc.ca**

BUY

PORTFOLIO

A few minutes of organizing your investment papers in an accordion-binder portfolio can save you heaps of hassle later on.

GOING PAPERLESS

READ • LISTEN • WATCH

NATURE OF THINGS
www.cbc.ca/natureofthings
David Suzuki's iconic long-running show will inspire you to preserve the beauty of Canada and the world's forests and wilderness.

PLANET EARTH: FORESTS
dsc.discovery.com/convergence/
planet-earth/guide/forests-02.
html
Check out this amazing documentary series from the BBC and the Discovery Channel that explores the power, complexity and threat to the world's forests.

ACT

PLANT A TREE
evergreen.ca
Take your paperless efforts to the next level by planting a tree for the future. Check out the Canadian-based Evergreen's database for information on planting your own tree and native tree species that will best flourish in your community.

DOUBLE-SIDED PRINTING
It only takes a second to hit the double-sided print button and you've cut your paper usage in half.

STOP JUNK MAIL
Post a notice on your mailbox specifying that you no longer want to receive unaddressed ad mail.

BUY

EREADERS
Whether Kindle, iPad, Kobo or otherwise, try out a paper-free version of your favourite book with these handy, digital readers.

PAPERLESS SUBSCRIPTIONS
More mags and newspapers are offering online subscriptions to their content. You can save heaps of papery goodness if you spring for this option instead.

BE A PHILANTHROPIST

READ • LISTEN • WATCH

IMAGINE CANADA'S ETHICAL CODE HANDBOOK
imaginecanada.ca
Before donating read up on the ethics a charitable organization should follow at Imagine Canada's online handbook.

CHARITY NAVIGATOR
charitynavigator.org
Check out this online search engine that ranks the practices of thousands of Canadian and American charities.

CHARITY VILLAGE
charityvillage.com/cv/
charityvillage/donfaq.html
The Craigslist of the non-profit world, this helpful site has a massive directory of organizations and information for volunteers and donors. However, you may still want to confirm independently the information you find here.

ACT

ONLINE FUNDRAISING
crowdrise.com
firstgiving.com
givemeaning.com
Set up a website for your fundraising project on giving websites where potential donors can peruse your cause and donate little or large amounts.

PENNY JAR
Set up a jar for chump change in your workplace and home, placing it in a spot everyone passes through. Make sure to include a sign indicating where the change will be donated.

CANADAHELPS
canadahelps.org
This is a one-stop shop for giving to charities in Canada. The site comes with a complete listing of registered charities across Canada that makes it easy to track down your cause and donate, quickly and easily, online.

BUY

MICROLOANS
globalgiving.com
kiva.org
freethechildren.com
For as little as a $20 loan you can help small projects in local communities get off the ground and make a big difference.

GIVING THE BIG & SMALL

READ • LISTEN • WATCH

HOW TO BE AN EVERYDAY PHILANTHROPIST
nicolebouchardboles.com
This book has over 300 non-monetary tips to make the world a better place, including dontating fat tissue (ew!).

365 WAYS TO CHANGE THE WORLD
365act.com
This British book provides a daily

way to make a difference, from giving someone a hug to learning self-defense.

TONIC
tonic.com
An empowering website that inspires you to log your good deeds, however big or small. You can offer things such as uploading an inspiring photo or sending out a fundraising tweet.

ACT

SCHEDULE A PICK-UP
diabetes.ca/clothesline
Organizations, such as Clothesline at Canadian Diabetes Association, will come right to your doorstep to pick up donations of shoes, toys, kitchen stuffs and more.

LOOK ONLINE
freecycle.org
craigslist.ca
Check out messageboards, such as FreeCycle or Craigslist's free listings, to find a home for your more random donations.

DONATE SPACE, DRIVING
Owning a large vehicle can have its socially conscious perks: offer your home as a drop-off place for goods and then do one major haul to a charity in need.

CUT YOUR HAIR
acvf.ca
Every year thousands of Canadians lose their hair from a variety of causes. Donating your hair to make a wig can save the cost and boost the confidence of someone in need. You can even mail your donation to the national

org, A Child's Voice Foundation.

DONATE YOUR WHEELS
charitycar.ca
Getting rid of your car could be the best thing you do for the environment and for someone else. Many charities are in need of vehicles to better deliver their services.

HOST A DRIVE
charityvillage.com
If there's a need for a certain something in your community (books for schools, old gadgets, mattresses), hold a drive for that item at work or a community centre. Check out Charity Village's complete cross-country listings for what organizations need.

THE JOY OF WALKING

READ • LISTEN • WATCH

THE DEATH AND LIFE OF GREAT AMERICAN CITIES
A seminal book from urban planner Jane Jacobs outlines many of the sustainable ideas of walkable cities still in use today.

CANADA WALKS
canadawalks.ca
A great online resource for all things bipedal, with walking maps, activist groups and studies on the benefits of walking.

SPACING MAGAZINE
spacing.ca
This unique magazine explores those overlooked urban areas with insightful articles on dead space or city rules. The publication has also spun out

into multiple city blogs devoted to Toronto, Montreal, Ottawa and the Atlantic provinces.

ACT

WALKSCORE
walkscore.com
A handy online tool that rates your community's walkability by nearby amenities: grocery stores, schools, movie theatres, libraries, parks and everything else a healthy community needs.

JANE'S WALK
janeswalk.net
This grassroots event every May that takes place in dozens of communities across Canada encourages people to lead or take an informational and exploratory walk around town. Be a tour guide and bring the Jane's Walk to your community.

WALKING TOURS
When visiting a new city, try taking a guided walking tour around some unique 'hoods, such as Manitoba's exchange district or Vancouver's Gastown.

STREET PARTIES
Ask around your street about organizing a street festival and shutting down your 'hood to cars for one day.

BUY

SMARTPHONE APPS
Make use of great (and cheap!) smartphone apps such as Yelp and Urbanspoon that give you precise information on great restaurants and other spots nearby.

A PET

Animals, dogs in particular, will get you out and exploring your neighbourhood and meeting new people. If you're not up for the commitment, offer to walk your neighbour's dog.

WALKING SHOES
mephisto.com
eccocanada.com

Feeling comfortable is essential to enjoying and continuing to walk. If you don't already own a pair, check out stylish yet practical brands such as ECCO and Mephisto.

BECOME A MENTOR

READ • LISTEN • WATCH

MENTORING CANADA
mentoringcanada.ca

This non-profit runs an online library and training portal for charities and organizations looking to set up a mentoring program. Look here for more information on mentoring links across the country.

HUFFINGTON POST LIVING, ADELE SCHEELE
huffingtonpost.com/adele-scheele

This *Huffington Post* columnist writes regularly on mentor-related topics, such as your using your vacation to find a vocation or how to find a mentor.

CITIES OF MIGRATION
citiesofmigration.ca

Helpful for those mentoring a newly landed immigrant to Canada, this experimental website showcases game-changing ideas and practices from the top cities of migration around the world, from Auckland, New Zealand to Paris, France to Hamilton, Ontario. You can peruse webinars, lecture series and articles from some of the top thinkers here.

ACT

SIGN UP
alliescanada.ca/find-your-iec

Join the national mentoring initiative from ALLIES (Assisting Local Leaders with Immigrant Employment Services) that has local Immigrant Employment Councils (IECs) in major cities across Canada. Don't see your city? Start your own mentoring chapter.

KEEP YOUR EYES PEELED (YOUR EARS, TOO!)

Listen to the needs of people in your community. This will yield tons of informal mentor and mentee opportunities in your community.

CANADA INFONET
canadainfonet.org

An online mentoring site for new and established Canadians.

YOUTH MENTORING
bgccan.com
girlguides.ca
scouts.ca
bigbrothersbigsisters.ca

There is a host of possible places to give aspiring youth a leg up. Check out Big Brothers, Big Sisters of Canada, Scouts Canada, Girl Guides of Canada and the Boys and Girls Club of Canada.

FEMALE ROLE MODELS
wil.ca

The Women in Leadership Foundation runs a 6-month mentorship program for women, designed to get more females into roles of leadership and management in Vancouver, Montreal and Toronto. Find out how to get involved here.

ON-CAMPUS MENTORING

Many universities have a Centre for Teaching and Learning for first-year students, international exchange students or those with disabilities. Check here for ways you can help provide mentorship or guidance.

BUY

GIVE A GIFT

Show your mentor or mentee you care by giving a personal gift to show your support or offer encouragement.

BUSINESS CARDS

Keeping cards with all your contact information will come in handy during your search for a mentorship role. If you meet someone who fits the bill, share your card and suggest meeting up.

BEYOND THE BALLOT BOX

READ • LISTEN • WATCH

APATHY IS BORING
apathyisboring.com

This Montreal-based group provides web and print resources to Canadian youth about the electoral process and political system.

LOCAL MOTION: THE ART OF CIVIC ENGAGEMENT IN TORONTO
chbooks.com
Through the lens of one city, this book of essays takes on how we can inspire change at a grass-roots level.

POWER AND POLITICS
cbc.ca/programguide/program/power_politics_with_evan_solomon
This weekday evening news show on CBC provides a regular briefing on the politics of the day and its effect on people, all guided by revered journalist Evan Solomon.

THE AGENDA WITH STEVE PAIKIN
tvo.org
Every weeknight on TVO, the hyper-literate Steve Paikin breaks down politics, media, the environment and foreign affairs. If you can't catch the broadcast, grab the podcast version of the show to listen to on the go.

WATCH QUESTION PERIOD
cpac.ca.
Federal, provincial and municipal proceedings are broadcast online. Keep up-to-date on an issue by tuning in and watching the discussion unfold. For federal, check out The Cable Public Affairs Channel at cpac.ca. For provincial and municipal, check out provincial and municipal websites for broadcasting information online.

ACT

START A PETITION
tigweb.org
Use online tools to create your own petition and bring attention to an important issue. Try Facebook's online petition tool or websites, such as Taking It Global.

START A CONVERSATION
Changing someone's mind often occurs during an open-minded conversation, rather than heated debate, trump speeches or ad campaigns. Whether this discussion occurs online or in person, keep the discussion healthy, informed and open.

ATTEND A MEETING
Get out to public hearings and community meetings, where you can ask questions, meet other passionate advocates and demonstrate to representatives that people care about these issues.

CALL YOUR REPRESENTATIVE
Get the email address or phone number of your federal, provincial and municipal representatives and contact them regularly about the issues you care about. Federal: canada.gc.ca/directories-repertoires, Provincial/Municipal: check the corresponding website.

STUDENT VOTE
For youth under the age of 18, you can register your school in the Student Vote, which takes place before federal and provincial elections, teaching the value and process of participating in democracy.

USE YOUR TALENT
Whatever your talent, use it to make a statement of your beliefs. Draw up a political cartoon, write a protest song or start a blog.

PEACEFUL, CREATIVE PROTEST
Engage your like-minded creative pals to get a point across in a peaceful, though pointed way. Express yourself on witty placards and try out wacky, attention-grabbing costumes.

JOIN THE CLUB
Many university campuses have student groups for political parties or start your own activist group to tackle big protest projects together.

PRACTICE MAKES PERFECT
Practice speaking and writing skills to better express your opinions.

LEARN ABOUT DEMOCRACY
Canada has a parliamentary democracy, but there are many versions around the world. Take time to learn the pros and cons of another country's system.

ACT

SCRAPBOOK
Keep a collection of clippings that relate to an issue you're following.

CRAFT MATERIALS
Make an attention-grabbing poster or enhance a petition with stickers, sparkles, sharpies and billboards.

BUTTON MACHINE

Invest in a button machine to dispense your own political messages. Need a cheaper alternative? Make your own stickers.

MEGAPHONE

long-mcquade.com
audiosoundselectronics.com

You can purchase a megaphone online from Audio Sound Electronics (from $60 to $100 depending on shipping) or rent one from Long & McQuade, the music store with locations across Canada.

SHARING HEALTH

READ • LISTEN • WATCH

CANADIAN BLOOD SERVICES

www.bloodservices.ca

Read up on the rules of who can donate and when before you roll up your sleeve.

ACT

GROW A 'STACHE

movember.ca

Movember started in Melbourne, Australia and quickly spread around the world, where it became incredibly popular in Canada. Hairy (and not-so-hairy) dudes can raise awareness and funds for prostate cancer through the month of November by sporting a 'stache.

TELL SOMEONE

Have a discussion early with friends and family about donating your body after death.

DONATE MILK

hmbana.org

Breast is best, but some women, for varying reasons, can't produce. Vancouver currently has the only breast milk bank in Canada (www.bcwomens.ca), but more are in the works for Quebec and Ontario. Check the Human Milk Banking Association of North America (HMBANA) for current listings of the nearest milk bank.

CUT YOUR HAIR

acvf.ca

Donate your hair to a child who has suffered from hair loss and in need of a little self-confidence through the national non-profit, A Child's Voice Foundation.

GIVE SIGHT

onesight.org

Check out ways to donate sight to someone in need, through programs such as OneSight, that facilitate second-hand eyeglass shipments to developing countries, among other programs.

GIVE (OR LOAN) MEDICAL EQUIPMENT

www.redcross.ca

Charities accept new or nearly new medical equipment such as wheelchairs and even medications. Check out Team Canada Healing Hands for more information (www.tchh.org) or Red Cross which accepts loans of various medical equipment.

SKILL SWAP

READ • LISTEN • WATCH

VOLUNTEER.CA

This is the website for all things

volunteering including a blog of inspiring stories as well as a database with links to the closest volunteer centre.

ACT

MATCH YOUR SKILLS

getinvolved.ca

Check out the Get Involved volunteer matching site that lists hundreds of organizations, from music festivals to rodeos, in need of certain skills to make something special happen.

LEARN FIRST AID & CPR

redcross.ca

Breathe new life into your CPR creds with a quick weekend course. You could save someone's life.

BABYSIT

Brush up on your babysitting skills and offer to watch a neighbour's tykes so a tired couple can have a date night.

LISTEN

culturelink.ca

Don't think you have any skills to donate? Tons of people only need a compassionate person to sit and listen. Check out organizations such as CultureLInk, which hooks up new immigrants with established Canadians.

BUY

A FAVOURITE BOOK

If someone's sick or in the hospital, pick up a copy of their favourite book or offer to read or record the book for them to listen to.

GROCERIES, ESSENTIALS

Everyday tasks can become insurmountable during a time of crisis. Offer to do a grocery run or feed a pet when a neighbour, friend or family member is in need.

RAISE YOUR VOICE

READ • LISTEN • WATCH

SOCIAL MEDIA FOR SOCIAL GOOD: A HOW-TO GUIDE FOR NONPROFITS

This new book by Heather Mansfield describes how non-profits can harness the power of social media for good. Learn some tricks here yourself.

MASHABLE'S TWITTER GUIDEBOOK
mashable.com/guidebook/twitter/

Popular tech blog Mashable keeps an extensive resource guide on how to best use Twitter for whatever your needs are.

MOVEMENTS.ORG
movements.org

This non-profit hosts a variety of conferences, meet-ups and summits on networking for grassroots digital activists, while its regularly updated blog keeps track of how social movements are leveraging social media.

ACT

SET A QUOTA

Promise yourself to pass along a set amount of articles relevant to your cause through social media every day.

FOLLOW OR FRIEND YOUR REPRESENTATIVE

Most MPs and MPPs are linked into the Internet, which means you can get daily updates on their activities simply by signing into Facebook or Twitter. Try to communicate directly with your rep by tweeting back or posting on his or her wall.

GET AN ONLINE COMMUNITY

Many blog platforms, such as Blogger, Wordpress, Tumblr, Foursquare et al., make it easy for you to post your thoughts and find other bloggers like you.

POST LIVE UPDATES

If you attend a rally, public hearing or community meeting, live blog or tweet updates to your community to keep those who can't attend in the loop.

ORGANIZE YOUR PLATFORMS
tweetdeck.com
hootsuite.com
cotweet.com
friendorfollow.com

Check out tools such as TweetDeck, HootSuite, CoTweet and others to simultaneously post to your different profile pages.

FLASH MOB
freethechildren.com/getinvolved/youth/campaigns

During election times, organize a vote mob with online friends to create excitement around participating in the vote. Or

gather a group of friends online to participate in Free The Children's Vow of Silence campaign, where activists stay silent for set period of time in support of a certain cause.

STRATEGIZE FOR SOCIAL MEDIA

Are you eager to raise awareness of a social issue, protest or event? Don't forget about social media to coalesce support for your project or issue. Create an event page on Facebook with eye-catching profile pictures, regular postings to interesting articles or links.

VOLUNTEER YOUR TALENTS

Have you got social media savvy? Offer your skills to a non-profit or charity in need of a little expertise managing a Twitter account or blogging about a fundraiser.

RAISE FUNDS ONLINE
crowdrise.com

Have a great cause but no funds to get it started? Check out Crowdrise, which provides fundraising pages to help you give your project a start.

BUY

A PASSWORD MANAGER

Keep track of your passwords for different social media sites, some of which are free, while others come with fees for protection. Roboform, at $29.95 for pro edition, free for regular: www.roboform.com., Lastpass, at lastpass.com, for $1 per month for premium account.

STAYCATION

READ • LISTEN • WATCH

AUDIO BOOKS
Download a book on tape that complements the area you're exploring. You can give yourself your own history lesson or learn about the underground culture of a place.

LOCAL WEEKLIES, BLOGS
straight.com
vueweekly.com
thecoast.ca

If you're travelling to a new city in Canada, you've gotta read what the locals do to find the unique activities. There's *The Straight* in Vancouver, *The Coast* in Halifax or *The Vue* in Edmonton among others.

ACT

HOBBY BINGE
Explore the familiar through the lens of a favourite hobby, whether that's paragliding, design or food.

SLOW DOWN
Get out to a new area by bicycle or on foot – you'll see more than if you speed up in a car. Alternatively, you can drive to a faraway spot and then hop out to start a wander.

TUNE IN
Take off your headphones and immerse yourself in the sounds of the scene.

INVITE VISITORS
couchsurfing.org
Make your house available to visiting friends and family or sign up to the Couchsurfing website where international travelers crash at your place. Acting as host can help reinvigorate your own experience of your city.

GROUP FUN
Plan a big outing with friends to a movie, musical or club. Going as a gang can seriously up the fun factor and transform a typical Friday night.

GO SMALL
Check out the tiny community museums, volunteer-run galleries, town halls, churches or heritage homes during your adventure off the beaten path. You're more likely to avoid crowds, pay less and also find some real hidden gems.

VOLUNTEER
Help out with an arts festival or street fair and you'll get free access to the offering as well as the opportunity to meet new people and see a different side of the city.

BUY

CITY PASSES
Many cities offer discounted passes that grant access to all the top attractions in town – purchasing one can save heaps and push you to try everything.

TRANSIT GROUP PASS
Look into a cheap, accessible way to get around town, such as family or group transit passes.

SEE THE WORLD

READ • WATCH • LISTEN

EAT PRAY LOVE
This best-selling tale of a woman's search for meaning through Italy, India and Indonesia has inspired many to hit the dusty trail in search of personal exploration.

MY ME TO WE TRIP
metowe.com
Designed for Me to We Volunteer Trips, this journal features excellent tips for interacting with foreign cultures and dealing with culture shock as well as space for thoughts and impressions.

PLANET EARTH
bbcearth.com
Watching these engaging BBC documentaries will get you excited about seeing, and also saving, the world.

ACT

RENEW YOUR PASSPORT
www.ppt.gc.ca
Having an up-to-date passport means you'll be much more likely to hop on a plane and get the heck out of town.

SHARE YOUR EXPERIENCE
Pick a way to share your thoughts and impressions with your friends and family far away: try a mailing list, a blog, zine or vlog.

WRITE A LETTER TO YOURSELF
Send a letter to yourself back home to remember a special moment of your trip. You'll treasure this memento when you come back home.

EXCHANGE INFORMATION
Keep in touch with new-found friends on your trip by finding

each other on social networks later or through email or good old fashioned letters.

BUY

A JOURNAL
Document your trip with writing. Or get creative and post in mementos you pick up along the way or photos you take or signatures you collect.

VOLUNTOURING

READ • WATCH • LISTEN

WORLD LITERATURE
Going to the Scottish Highlands? Pack some Walter Scott into your trunk. Heading to India? Pick up Rohinton Mistry's *A Fine Balance*. Reading the literature inspired by a country will get you excited to immerse yourself in a new world.

INTO THE WILD
Pretty much all of John Krakauer's books will make you feel like a slouch, but this break-through novel will compel you to explore the world.

ACT

CANADIAN YOUTH VOLUNTEER TRIPS
katimavik.org
Katimavik is government-run program that enrolls youth between the ages of 17 and 21 in six months of life-changing volunteer service, placing you in two diverse communities across the country.

ORGANIC FARMING
wwoof.org
Check out WWOOF, which stands for World Wide Opportunities on Organic Farms, an international listing of volunteer placements that offer food and board in exchange for labour.

ME TO WE TRIPS
metowe.com/trips
Go on a Me to We trip to one of the five countries where we build schools, water systems and alternative income projects.

SKILLED VOLUNTEER TRIPS
cuso-vso.org
CUSO-VSO sends skilled volunteers, with over two years working experience, overseas to help foreign charities in need of expertise.

RAISE SOME ROOFS
Habitat for Humanity provides both long-term and short-term volunteer trips.

BUY

A BACKPACK
Invest in some sturdy equipment, such as a good backpack, to get you out on the road, exploring the world and giving back.

A SLEEPING BAG
Get ready to make your bed wherever you travel.

TREAD LIGHTLY

READ • WATCH • LISTEN

THE ETHICAL TRAVEL GUIDE
earthscan.co.uk
This exhaustive guide from the international travel org EarthScan provides listings for ethical getaway spots on five continents.

TRAVELANTHROPIST
travelanthropist.com
Check out this site for stories, trip ideas and articles on responsible tourism.

GROUNDED: A DOWN TO EARTH JOURNEY AROUND THE WORLD
sethstevenson.com
Two thirty-somethings pack all their belongings into storage and set off for a trip around the world - the only rule: no planes. Although the trip isn't necessarily about carbon output (the couple ride all manner of transportation, from steam ships to trains) the tale is an inspiring take on the benefits of slower, scenic travel.

ACT

DITCH THE WHEELS
As soon as you hit your destination, get rid of the car and use public transportation, rentable bikes or scooters. You'll save money and get an up-close experience of the surroundings.

FOLLOW THE TRAIL
While visiting natural areas, make sure to stay on the designated trail, so as not to trample wildlife and to avoid nettles or poison ivy, and refrain from littering. This will keep the setting beautiful for the next visitor.

GREEN HABITS

Don't ditch your conscientious habits while you're away: turn off lights when you leave your room, reuse towels, skip the mini plastic shampoo bottles in place of bringing your own and bring a reusable water bottle or coffee mug with you.

LOCAL GIFTS

Search out gifts made by locals, rather than those shipped in from outside manufacturers. It helps support the local economy and leaves you with an authentic souvenir of your travels.

BUY

CARBON OFFSETS
less.ca

Look into carbon offsetting your train, bus or plane travel for wherever you're headed. Check out Less, an Ecologo-certified and independently audited carbon offset provider.

HYBRID VEHICLE RENTALS

If renting a vehicle is part of your travel plans, look into a hybrid or more fuel-efficient model to keep your impact light.

ECO-HOTEL ROOM
greenkeyglobal.com
trailcanada.com

Search out eco-friendly hotels that are certified as having a lower impact on the earth, through water conservation, natural cleaners, recycled paper and more. Check out the Green Key Rating System or Trail Canada.

BECOME A PEN PAL

READ • WATCH • LISTEN

FOREIGN CORRESPONDENCE: A PEN PAL'S JOURNEY FROM DOWN UNDER TO ALL OVER
geraldinebrooks.com

Get inspired by this memoir from Australian writer Geraldine Brooks as she recounts her experiences learning about the planet from pen pals around the world.

MY PEN PAL: THIS AMERICAN LIFE
thisamericanlife.org/radio-archives/episode/246/my-pen-pal

This popular podcast from NPR explores tales of very unusual pen pal relationships and their ability to break down barriers between people and cultures.

THE LETTER EXCHANGE
letter-exchange.com

This quarterly print publication connects people who want to write letters to other die-hard, snail-mail fans, by circulating a list of other devoted pen pals.

ACT

SEND A POSTCARD TO A STRANGER
postcrossing.com

Participate in the PostCrossings project: if you send a postcard to anyone in its database with over 5 million users from around the world, you'll receive one in return.

POST A LETTER SOCIAL ACTIVITY CLUB (PAL SAC)
pal-sac.com

This letter-writing club meets once a month to write letters on Pay-What-You-Can stationary. There are chapters across Canada (Toronto, Ottawa, Montreal, Vancouver and Brandon, MB), so you can either join or create your own.

SPEAK OUT

Send a letter to your local, provincial, territorial or federal representative, either commending them for speaking out on an issue or registering a complaint. One personalized letter can go a long way.

KEEP THE CONNECTION

Use Skype, Google Phone and other low-cost ways to keep in touch with friends and family far away.

BUY

FANCY PAPER, ENVELOPES

Buy some pretty paper to gussy up your envelopes and letters for pals far away.

STAMPS

Get a personalized stamp with your favourite quotes or symbols on them to make letter writing even more fun.

TUCK IN

Add an extra surprise to your mail: a friendship bracelet, fridge magnet, stickers or even a few extra postage stamps to encourage your pen pal to write you back promptly.

ESCAPE TO NATURE

READ • LISTEN • WATCH

LAST CHILD IN THE WOODS: SAVING OUR CHILDREN FROM NATURE DEFICIT DISORDER
richardlouv.com
Robert Louv's groundbreaking book introduced the concept of nature deficit disorder and stressed its importance to children's development.

LATE NIGHTS ON AIR
This award-winning novel by Elizabeth Hays is a great escape to the beauty of Canada's north, exploring the lives of radio broadcasters living and tripping through the Northwest Territories.

ASSOCIATION OF EXPERIENTIAL LEARNING
aee.org/re/resources
This organization has heaps of academic resources on the power of nature and adventure.

WATERWALKER
www.nfb.ca/film/waterwalker
You can watch Bill Mason's ultimate documentary on the beauty of Ontario's Great Lakes for free on the National Film Board's website.

THE NATURE OF THINGS
www.cbc.ca/natureofthings
Share Canadian icon David Suzuki's long-time love for the planet on this CBC-TV show.

ACT

OUTDOOR GETAWAYS
blackfeather.com
Ease yourself into a full-on adventure by going with an experienced tripping organization. Check out Blackfeather's entirely customizable trips that can be adjusted for small or large groups of families, or all-womens and depending on skill level and adventure type.

IMPOSSIBLE 2 POSSIBLE
impossible2possible.com
This Canadian non-profit takes school groups on challenging trips around the world and in Canada.

THE OTESHA PROJECT
otesha.ca
Take a socially conscious cycling tour across the Kootenay Mountains, the Sunshine Coast of British Columbia or a local food tour through Eastern Ontario, all focused on spreading the word about sustainable initiatives and engaging with the beauty of the country.

BUY

CAMPING GEAR
Invest in starter equipment (a tent, sleeping bag and camper stove) to get started on your outdoors adventures. Even if you're only a few feet from the car.

CHANNEL SURF
oln.ca
Subscribe to the Outdoor Life Network channel, where you can watch Canadian icon "Survivorman" tackle the coasts of Labrador or the dusty terrains of the Kalahari desserts.

CANADIAN GEOGRAPHIC
canadiangeographic.ca
Get this monthly magazine delivered to your doorstep and you'll be chockfull of ideas for getting outside and exploring the country.

AVOID THE WASH

READ • LISTEN • WATCH

ECOLABEL INDEX
ecolabelindex.com
Check out this cool site that explains all the environmental labels for you.

THE JOY OF GREEN CLEANING
greencleaningcoach.com
A wonderful collection of DIY recipes from Leslie Reichert for home-cleaning concoctions.

NATURAL HOME AND GARDEN MAGAZINE
naturalhomeandgarden.com
A magazine all about greener homes and cleaning.

SUSTAIN LANE
sustainlane.com
This busy hive of an online community is always buzzing with talk on green products, businesses, tips, information and coupons.

ACT

MAKE A "WHAT-NOT-TO-BUY" LIST
After doing your own research, write down a list of ingredients, products and brands that you should avoid when you hit the grocery store

START A BLOG
Share your experiences, tips, and reviews of cleaning products with a like-minded community online.

CLEAN THE OFFICE
Recommend the use of eco-friendly cleaning products and methods for the workplace or bring in your own supplies.

BUY

BAKING SODA, VINEGAR AND LEMON
These usual suspects in any pantry are a great start for cleaning naturally.

RECIPE BOX
Keep track of your cleaning recipes in one spot.

CONTAINERS AND LABELS
Make your cleaning easier by labeling all your home-made cleaning supplies and creating a special place for them.

HOME ENERGY AUDIT

READ • LISTEN • WATCH

HOLMES ON HOMES
holmeshomes.ca
This popular home improvement show with host-contractor Mike Holmes also incorporates solar technology, green roofs, grey water recycling and other sustainable building practices into its construction projects.

ECOHOLIC HOME
ecoholic.ca
Adia Vasil's fun and informative

book tells you everything you need to know about greening your home in Canada.

AZURE MAGAZINE
azuremagazine.com
Although this Toronto mag caters to a more designer crowd, there are many sustainable home improvements covered in the pages.

INHABITAT
inhabitat.com
This green design blog covers environmental issues from a design angle, with stories about the eco-benefits of innovative architecture, technology, energy use, fashion and more.

ACT

AUDIT THE HOMESTEAD
oee.nrcan.gc.ca
The sooner you get your house audited, the sooner you can save on energy and heating bills by sealing up drafts and conserving energy. Check out the Office of Energy Efficiency, run by Natural Resources Canada, for a list of grants and energy advisors in your area.

HABITAT FOR HUMANITY
habitat.ca
Volunteer with Habitat for Humanity, which builds houses for lower-income families. You can also donate unused paint and building materials to one of its ReStores across Canada.

CHECK THE WARRANTY
On every new product you buy for your home, check the warranty first and ensure the

company will take care of recycling the product at the end of its life.

BUY

CAULKING
A cheap and easy-to-use tube of caulking can quickly plug drafty holes around windows and doors.

PROGRAMMABLE THERMOSTAT
For less than a $100, you can get a thermostat that keeps track of your heating and cooling, saving you energy and money.

ECOLOGO PRODUCTS
ecologo.org
Whatever you're planning to purchase for your house, from toilets to fire logs to kitchen towels, check the EcoLogo certified product listings for the environmentally preferable option.

A GOOD NEIGHBOUR

READ • WATCH • LISTEN

THE GOOD NEIGHBOUR COOK BOOK
thegoodneighborcookbook.com
This recipe book offers 125 easy recipes that make it easy for you to surprise, console or welcome a neighbour.

BOWLING ALONE
Robert Putnam's influential book exposed the cracks in modern-day North American society and continues to inspire introspection into the decline of community today.

ACT

COOK SOMETHING
Where words and actions fail, some homemade comfort food (think gooey mac n' cheese or tomato soup) can bridge the gap.

FIX SOMETHING
If you're handy around the house, offer to pitch in cleaning out the roof gutters or painting a hard-to-reach corner.

HOST AN OPEN HOUSE
Open your home to newcomers or elderly neighbours for a potluck dinner or board game night.

EXCHANGE KEYS
Trade house keys with neighbours you trust and be there for one another if someone loses a key, needs help with pet care during vacation or simply needs their house watched while they're away.

BUY

FLOWERS
Get planters for your street to spruce up worn-down spaces.

A PICNIC TABLE
Sometimes all a street needs is a spot to sit and gab. Check first for prohibitive bylaws and then buy a picnic table gift the entire street can enjoy.

NATURAL CLEANERS

READ • WATCH • LISTEN

BETTER BASICS FOR THE HOME
anniebbond.com
This master compendium of recipes offers 800 less-toxic solutions for cleaning your home, as well as taking care of your body and garden.

MAKE YOUR PLACE
microcosmpublishing.com
This pocket-sized guide lists all sorts of information for natural shampoos, facial cleansers and, of course, home cleaners.

ACT

BREW UP A BATCH
Try these quick recipes for *au natural* home cleaning:

All-purpose cleaning spray: 2 parts water to 1 part white vinegar

Sink Cleaner: 1 cup vinegar to 1/2 cup baking soda

Drain Opener: Pour 1/2 cup baking soda down drain, followed by 1/2 cup vinegar

Toilet Cleaner: Sprinkle baking soda onto the rims of the toilet, follow by vinegar and scrub.

BUY

NATURAL CLEANING INGREDIENTS
Vinegar, borax, baking soda, salt, lemon juice, castile soap, essential oils and hydrogen peroxide.

MEASURING CUPS AND SPOONS
You may want to purchase a special batch of measuring tools for your cleaning ingredients.

LATEX GLOVES
Wear these when handling ingredients, such as Borax, which can irritate the skin.

SPRAY, SQUIRT BOTTLES
It's ideal to reuse old bottles, but you can also buy up a bunch to hold homemade cleaners.

A FUNNEL
After brewing up your batch of cleaner, a funnel will help you get the cleaner into a bottle easily.

HOME SHARE

ACT

SURF THE COUCH
couchsurfing.org
This popular website lets tourists and locals connect with people posting free spots to stay. The benefits of posting your own couch means you can meet a slew of interesting travelers passing through town and rediscover your own city.

HOST A FOREIGN STUDENT
canadahomestayinternational.com
Learn about a new culture and make a new friend by opening your home to foreign students. Families are often remunerated for the costs incurred. Check out Canadian International Student Services (www1.cisscanada.com) or the Canada Homestay Network.

DONATE A COTTAGE
cottagedreams.org
Charities, such as Cottage Dreams, allow cottage owners to donate their getaways to recovering cancer survivors.

LABELS AND SIGNS
Designate areas of your home that are shared or private.

ENTERTAINMENT
Invest in communal board games, movies or mini library to make a hang-out spot more comfortable and fun.

EATING TOGETHER

READ • WATCH • LISTEN

THE FAMILY DINNER: GREAT WAYS TO CONNECT WITH YOUR KIDS ONE MEAL AT A TIME
thefamilydinnerbook.com
Written by Laurie David, producer of *An Inconvenient Truth*, this book features recipes and tips to liven up the conversation with whomever is sitting at your table.

DINNER AT YOUR DOOR: TIPS AND RECIPES FOR STARTING A NEIGHBOURHOOD COOKING CO-OP
A great primer on how to start a food co-op in your 'hood.

BETTER TOGETHER
bettertogetherbc.ca
This blog and resource site, created by the BC Ministry of Health and the BC Dairy Foundation, is a great online space to share stories and tips on eating together.

LUNCH LOVE COMMUNITY
lunchlovecommunity.org
Dubbed an "open space documentary project," you can watch many inspiring short documentaries on healthy lunch habits for kids.

COOKING FOR THE RUSHED
cookingfortherushed.com
Sandy Richards, the host of the Food Network show *Fixing Dinner*, is passionate about getting busy families to make time to eat together. Her site is full of helpful one-minute cooking videos.

ACT

TELL A STORY
Rotate between family members, each bringing a story of their week or day to the table.

START A DINNER CO-OP
Start a dinner co-op with nearby friends and acquaintances whose cooking you admire. By meeting once a week and exchanging meals in Tupperware, you'll try out new recipes, strengthen community ties and spend less time slaving over the oven.

A FAVOURITE FOOD
Rotate favourite dishes throughout the week so each family member or guest has something special to look forward to.

GET THE KIDS COOKING
Young kids love to help in the kitchen and you can give them more and more responsibility as they get older. If a teen is complaining about food choices, instigate a new rule where he (or she) who cooks makes the menu.

BUY

PLACE MARKERS
Arrange, or even illustrate, special place setting markers to turn that weekday meal into a special event.

CANDLES AND FLOWERS
Don't forget atmosphere when planning romantic dinners.

LOCAL FOOD

READ

THE 100-MILE DIET: A YEAR OF LOCAL EATING
This seminal book, written by the Vancouver writing couple Alisa Smith and J.B. Mackinnon, sparked the 100-mile food movement and challenged eaters near and far to eat food within a set geographical limitation.

APPLES TO OYSTERS
www.margaretwebb.com
Food writer Margaret Webb eats her way across Canada in this excellent book about local food and farming.

LOCAL FOOD PLUS
localfoodplus.ca
Check out this blog that explores all local food issues in Canada.

SIMPLY IN SEASON
worldcommunitycookbook.org
Organized by season, this recipe book helps you pick local recipes based on what's in season.

ACT

GROW YOUR OWN
Fresh herbs on the windowsill, tomatoes and lettuce on the balcony, cucumbers, green

beans and radishes if you have a backyard: these are all easy to grow and delicious to eat.

FARMERS MARKETS CANADA
farmersmarketscanada.ca
Visit one of the 500 farmers markets across Canada selling fresh, local produce.

JOIN A CO-OP
coopscanada.coop
Over 200 food co-ops across Canada are involved with local food initiatives, making it easy to buy products from nearby.

ASK QUESTIONS
At farmers markets, ask vendors specific questions about where your food comes from and how far it travelled. Read the stickers and labels at the grocery store.

SEARCH OUT GREAT RECIPES
supernaturalrecipes.com
Run an ingredient through this Google-powered search engine, trained to track down natural, whole food recipes, and you'll soon be salivating over healthy dishes.

BUY

REUSABLE BAGS
Most vendors at farmers markets tend not to give away plastic bags. Bringing your own cuts down on waste.

GOOD FOOD BOX
foodshare.net
No time to hit the market? Look for a nearby good food box distributor (dozens are available across Canada) that distributes local and organic produce for cheap.

FOOD WASTE

READ

WASTE: UNCOVERING THE GLOBAL FOOD SCANDAL
tristramstuart.co.uk
British journalist Tristram Stuart tracks the roots of our global food waste problem and its effect on the developing countries and the environment.

LOVE FOOD, HATE WASTE
lovefoodhatewaste.com
The Brits are facing down the food waste problem with a government-sponsored website that features tips and tricks for reusing foodstuffs and reducing waste.

ACT

DONATE FRUIT AND VEGETABLES
If you have a tree sprouting a bumper crop of apples or monster zucchinis taking over your backyard, try donating some of this fresh produce to a local food bank in need of nutritious food.

FOOD WASTE FRIDAYS
Follow the lead of bloggers around the world who are weighing and photographing their food waste one day a week, with the hope of getting down to zero food waste.

MAKE MUFFINS
Find a basic recipe you like and tweak it to include leftover fruits or veggies you have. Great unlikely combos include zucchini and apple, carrot and pineapple, strawberry and banana. If you have too much, bring it to the office, and you'll make friends in no time.

CHILI CON CARNE
Any leftover meat can be thrown into this dish. Put remaining meat into a slow cooker with red kidney beans, onions, tomatoes and seasoning and you'll have a delicious dinner. Leftover veggies? Throw them in for a nutritious spin on an old classic.

BUY

JUICER/BLENDER
No more gouging out the mushy parts of a banana: churn up over-ripe fruit or veggies into a healthful smoothie or juice.

TUPPERWARE
Invest in quality containers to freeze whatever fruit and vegetables are mush-ifying. Preserve them for a later recipe instead.

FRIDGE POLICE APP
fridgepolice.com
This handy app allows you to keep track of all the expiry dates in your fridge by scanning the bar code with your smartphone.

FAMILY TRADITIONS

READ

VOLUNTEER.CA
This online resource about volunteering in all forms has a great listing of family volunteer ideas.

YES! MAGAZINE
yesmagazine.org
An online and a print magazine that empowers people to make positive social change.

THE BUSY FAMILY'S GUIDE TO VOLUNTEERING: DOING GOOD TOGETHER
doinggoodtogether.org
This book offers tons of tips and activity ideas for families looking to volunteer as a team.

ACT

ADOPT A FAMILY
hopeforchildren.ca
Contact this organization that runs an "Adopt-a-Family" program that matches up in-need families during the holidays and ensures that more children will receive a thoughtful gift.

CULTURE NIGHT
Cook a meal from a different country and watch a documentary on an important issue that the family can discuss after.

DINNER TOPICS
Bring up regular dinner topics at the table: did anyone witness a small injustice that day? What did you about it? Or, ask after any inspiring experiences of the day.

BUY

WALL CALENDAR
Organize your family's time to better tackle activities together.

SCRAPBOOK
Keep memories of the fun family time spent volunteering.

COLOUR-COORDINATED T-SHIRTS
This makes finding one another easy when volunteering in a large group.

MATERIAL WORLD

READ • LISTEN • WATCH

THE BERENSTAIN BEARS GET THE GIMMIES
This long-running children's book series tackles the usual problems faced by families in fun, lighthearted illustrations about this popular family of bears. This tale in particular takes on the common "gimmies" affliction most kids experience at one age or another.

CRAFTING A GREEN WORLD
craftingagreenworld.com
This do-it-yourself online hub for crafters provides kid-friendly instructions for presents, games and afternoon activities.

HOWTOONS
howtoons.com
This great website features instructional comics that encourage kids to take on fun and engaging projects at home.

ACT

GIVE REASONS
Before you automatically say "no" to friends' requests, pause and give a reason for why. Explain you're on a tight budget, it's unhealthy or that there's not enough time.

LEAD BY EXAMPLE
Refrain from buying things that you don't need as well.

ENCOURAGE CRITICAL THINKING
Ask your child to divide his or her shopping list into "needs" and "wants." Get them to explain why each request fits into a certain category.

RESEARCH CHILD LABOUR AND CONSUMERISM
Assign a short home research project on where a toy or t-shirt comes from, encouraging your child to explore child labour issues, conflict minerals, rampant consumerism or pollution.

FUN CHORES
Ask your child to help with tasks they enjoy, for instance cooking, creating table place settings or gardening chores.

BUY-NOTHING CHALLENGES
Challenge the whole family to refrain from purchasing anything besides groceries and transportation for one week. Seek out other ways to have fun instead.

BUY

BUY SOMETHING FOR SOMEONE ELSE
Instead of buying something for yourself or for your child, encourage your child to get something that a friend or another family member needs.

FAIR TRADE PRODUCTS
Spend a few extra dollars on the fair-trade version of your favourite chocolate, tea or coffee and know that somewhere someone's life is a little easier.

GIFTS THAT GIVE BACK

Check out companies, such as TOMs shoes (www.tomsshoes.ca) or Me to We Books, that give a pair of shoes or a book for every one sold.

GIFT + PASSION

READ

THE WORLD NEEDS YOUR KID
www.metowe.com

Our book about raising compassionate children offers many more techniques and tips to parents about how to inspire your child.

LESSONS FROM A STREET KID
www.metowe.com

This children's book, written by Craig, tells the story of a simple lesson he learned from a boy who had nothing and gave everything.

ACT

TAX CREDITS
cra-arc.gc.ca/fitness

Did you know you could get up to $500 per child for enrollment in a sports program? Check out tax breaks that fuel your kids' passion.

ENCOURAGE TOUGH QUESTIONS

Kids can say the darndest things! Let your child know, through words and body language, that you're open to answering any and all of their questions.

BUST AN AD

Deconstruct a billboard ad or TV commercial with your kids by asking pointed questions about who the ad is directed at, what it's selling and what the ad is suggesting the product will do for the consumer.

BUY

PIZZA

A little pizza goes a long way, especially when it comes to feeding a gang of hungry world changers eager to pursue socially conscious activities. Help support their efforts by purchasing the pizza, snacks or other treats.

A WORLD MAP

Hang a map in your child's room or in another room of the house with high traffic. When bringing up social justice issues around the house, ask them to identify what part of the world this issue is happening in, and what other countries it may affect.

RANDOM ACT OF KINDNESS

READ • LISTEN • WATCH

OPERATION NICE
operationnice.com

This blog posts regular stories of people going out of their way to do a stranger a favour. There are also plenty of ideas for how you can brighten someone's day.

PAY IT FORWARD

This Hollywood flick tells the inspiring story of a young boy who embarks on a mission to make the world a better place through small acts of kindness.

TONIC.COM

This website posts a slew of positive, psychologically based stories. Each story comes with a "Do Good" button, encouraging readers to do a good act right now, such as posting a positive Facebook update or thanking your father (or father figure) for life lessons he taught you.

ACT

COMMUTER ETIQUETTE

Give up your seat on the bus or train to someone in need. Offer to give a neighbour a ride to work or help someone cross the street.

ALL-WEATHER FRIEND

Offer to share your umbrella when someone is getting drenched, shovel your neighbour's driveway during the winter or offer someone a sealed bottle of water during the summer

BE AWARE

Notice someone is stressed or anxious while waiting in line? Let them go ahead. See someone struggling in their purse for change? Offer a quarter. Being aware of your surroundings means you're more able to see when someone needs a hand.

GIVE THANKS ONLINE

Compliment someone on Facebook or Twitter, remember someone's birthday with a quick message or wish someone luck on a job interview.

START A CONVERSATION

Take a minute to chat with a bus driver, barista or someone you usually rush through your interaction with.

CARDS
Keep a pretty set of cards handy to leave a kind message for someone who needs a little pick-me-up.

CHANGE POUCH
Keep spare change with you in case you encounter someone in need.

JOKE BOOK
A book of comics, cheesy one-liners or favourite jokes can help brighten your day.

KIDS BOOKS

READ

THE GIVING TREE
This classic story about friendship tells the tale of a boy and a tree. As the boy grows up, his needs keep changing and the tree keeps giving until one day, there seems to be nothing left for the tree to give.

CHILDREN AROUND THE WORLD
Teaching lessons in global community, this informational picture book explores the themes of commonality and diversity from the perspective of 12 children from different parts of the world.

LOVE YOU FOREVER
This classic Canadian children's book tells the story of love through the lives of a parent and child.

THE LORAX
Another classic children's book from Seussville, this one with an environmental message, tells the tale of the Lorax, the Once-ler and disappearing habitat.

ACT

SUGGEST A BOOK
Don't see books with substantial messages in the library or classroom? Bring a list of friendly suggestions to the librarian or teacher in charge. Or donate your own library.

WRITE YOUR OWN BOOK
There are millions of stories of compassion that still need to be told. Break out that pen and write your own.

RESEARCH & READ
Look up a word or research a topic that you don't understand or that interests you while you're reading.

START A BOOK CLUB
Share and discuss your favourite books with other parents and kids, supplementing the book with an open dialogue about what the message might be.

READ FOR YOURSELF
Make time for reading your own booklist at night or the newspaper in the morning. Setting this example for your kids is the best encouragement they can get.

BUY

BOOK LIGHT
Getting shut-eye is important, but

encouraging a love of reading is, too.

BOOKSHELF
Install a bookshelf in your child's room to fuel his or her inner book worm.

JOURNAL
Keep a journal nearby while reading to take down notes and inspirational quotes.

POST-IT NOTES
Bookmark words, concepts and plots that you don't understand or want to explore more.

BULLY ALERT

READ

STOP A BULLY – CANADIAN ANTI-BULLYING SCHOOL PROGRAM
stopabully.ca
This site provides helpful resources, such as victim support letters and anti-bullying posters, for Canadian children experiencing or rallying against bullying at school.

STAND UP 2 BULLYING
redcross.ca/StandUp
Developed by the Red Cross, this anti-bullying site provides statistics, tips and resources on combating bullying and raising awareness.

ACT

WEAR PINK
pinkshirtday.ca
Anti-bullying days vary across the country (British Columbia: April 14, Nova Scotia: February 23), so

find the right date and make sure to show your support with pink garb.

DON'T STAND BY
kidshelpphone.ca
Get comfortable with reporting and speaking up against bullying when you witness it.

BE A SYMPATHETIC EAR
Reach out to classmates or co-workers in need of venting after experiencing bullying or any kind of difficult episode.

START A BULLYING PREVENTION PROGRAM
Start an anti-bullying workshop, host a support group or create a bullying awareness week at school or in the workplace.

BE AWARE
Train yourself to spot different forms of bullying, as well as the stereotypes and misconceptions that can encourage bullying.

DONATE AND VOLUNTEER
kidshelpphone.ca
The phones at Kids Help Phone are staffed by professional counselors, however, you can help fundraise or donate to keep those counselors available to kids in need.

CREATE "NO BULLY ZONE" SIGNS
Place these signs in strategic places at school or work to let everyone know bullying is not tolerated.

BUY

CUPCAKES
Diffuse a tense workplace or classroom with treats.

BOARD GAMES
Create a friendlier atmosphere by introducing fun games and other team-bonding activities.

PET RESCUE

READ • LISTEN • WATCH

FOUND DOGS: TALES OF STRAYS WHO LANDED ON THEIR FEET
founddogs.com
Full of inspiring stories of dogs lost and found and how it changes the lives of both owner and pet. Also, great photography by Diana Walker.

DOGSTER, CATSTER
**dogster.com,
catster.com**
This massive and proliferating online forum has an extensive adoption section and tons of tips and suggestions for adopting animals.

ACT

ORGANIZE A PET-TRAINING WORKSHOP
Invite a pet-shelter worker to speak at your workplace to answer any questions or dispel any myths around adopting animals.

VOLUNTEER
Contact your local SPCA to find out how you can volunteer with animals on a regular basis.

FOSTER PARENT
Shelters are often in need of short-term care for animals with special needs. Contact your local SPCA to find out how to qualify and offer assistance.

REPORT STRAY ANIMALS
If you see what seems like a stray or lost animal wandering through your neighbourhood, take the time to report it to your local shelter. The animal could be lost, in need of medical attention or carrying disease.

SPONSOR A PET
soardogrescue.ca/sponsor.php
For just $5 a month you can sponsor a stray dog's housing and feeding costs until it finds a loving home.

BUY

PETFINDER
phunware.com/apps/discovery-communications-petfinder/
Get this free app for your phone to peruse adoption listings on the go.

MICROCHIP
Consider getting a microchip for your pet.

PET-PROOF YOUR HOME
This could include fencing in your yard, getting rid of chewable wires and poisonous plants as well as creating a cosy spot for your pet to hang out in.

GARDEN SHARE

READ

YOU GROW GIRL
yougrowgirl.com
A blog from Toronto-based garden writer Gayla Trail for those with big gardening dreams, but little space.

NORTH AMERICAN NATIVE PLANT SOCIETY
nanps.org
Check out this informative website about planting native fauna and flora that require less water.

LANDSHARE CANADA
landsharecanada.com
Similar to sharingbackyards.com, this cross-country network links up growers and sharers of space online. Also, the helpful blog offers heaps of information for getting started.

ACT

SCHEDULE YOUR TIME
If there are certain times you would like your garden all to yourself, consider creating a schedule to better share your space with others.

COMMUNITY GARDEN
Many Canadian cities have community garden plots scattered throughout the municipality. If you're not ready to tend one on your own, split the work (and the bounty) with a gardening pal.

GUERRILLA GARDEN
guerrillagardening.org
Not entirely legal, but this act of beautifying public space with a bit of greenery can turn a neglected patch of dirt into a flowering garden.

AVOID LITTERING
Collecting up your trash after a picnic means the next picnickers can enjoy a pristine space and animals won't eat plastic or other indigestible leftovers.

TEND A NEIGHBOUR'S GARDEN
Summer is not only peak gardening period, it's also time for vacation-taking as well. Offer to care for someone's garden or water their plants while they're away.

BUY

HEIRLOOM SEEDS
twowingsfarm.com
There is a wide and wonderful world of tasty and unique looking produce out there, from purple beans to devilish-looking tomatoes, with online seed catalogues across the country.

GARDENING TOOLS
Invest in a few hardy tools (a tilling tool, hose and gloves) to help make your green time easier.

GIFTS THAT GIVE BACK

READ

START SOMETHING THAT MATTERS
tomsshoes.ca
Blake Mycoskie, founder of the popular TOMs shoe company that gives a pair of shoes to a child in need for every pair sold, shares his ideas for making all facets of life more charitable.

CHARITABLE GIFT GIVING
charitablegiftgiving.com
This blog keeps track of all the latest gifts that contribute to charity or other social causes.

UNBOWED
greenbeltmovement.org
This detailed autobiography from Nobel Peace Prize winner and environmental activist Wangari Maathai makes a great gift. It tells her story of triumph and struggle through the decades of Kenya's dictatorship and final push for democracy.

ACT

GIVE A BOOK
Every time you open a book, there's the chance to learn something new. Seek out non-fiction books that explore an issue, such as climate change, the financial crisis or the in-depth history of one country.

LEARN SOMEONE'S PASSION
Give a friend or family member a gift that speaks to his or her interests.

ASK AND GIVE DONATIONS
Instead of material items, ask for donations to a cause or contribute in someone's name yourself.

COLLECTIVE GIFTS
Pool a gift donation with extended family members or your workplace to make a greater impact to a cause.

BUY

ME TO WE ARTISANS
metowe.com
From beautifully embroidered leather belts to stamped sterling earrings inspired by Maasai Mara design, each piece of Me to We Artisans jewelry supports the Kenyan mamas who craft these beautiful pieces.

FREE THE CHILDREN GIFT CATALOG
freethechildren.com/donate/gifts
There are plenty of donations that are fitting for a Christmas gift up or larger bequest. From $25 for a school kit, $50 for a goat and up to $5,000 for a community well.

NEST
buildanest.com
This artisanal jewelry site operates through microbartering: interest-free loans are provided to women in developing countries who then craft the items available for sale on the site. You can either purchase from women overseas or from US-based designers in the Nest network, the proceeds of which go toward Nest's mission.

OXFAM UNWRAPPED
oxfamunwrapped.ca
Similar to Free The Children's gift catalogue, Oxfam provides a variety of gift options, tailored to a passion, interest or occasion.

EVERGREEN
evergreen.ca
A national organization that fosters green spaces in cities across Canada. Symbolic gifts provide gardening workshops for teens, summer camp for inner-city kids or bean-keeper kits for youth.

FEEL-GOOD GIFTS

READ

29 GIFTS: HOW A MONTH OF GIVING CAN CHANGE YOUR LIFE
29gifts.org
This book tells the inspiring story of a woman suffering from multiple sclerosis, who uses the power of giving and receiving gifts to change her life and outlook. This *New York Times* bestseller evolved into a challenge that now has an accompanying website to share and discuss how giving has changed your life.

CRAFT MAGAZINE
craftzine.com
Knitting, sewing, jewellery, woodworking and all other forms of crafting can be found in this handy online magazine.

READYMADE
readymade.com
Check out this print mag and its wonderful blog of inspiring projects that are easy to turn into gifts. Who wouldn't want cinnamon ice cream or an iPod carrying case made with love?

INSTRUCTABLES
instructables.com
A slew of fun projects, along with clear instructions, that can easily make a great gift, such as home-fermented kimchi or funky patio chairs.

ACT

SLEUTH SKILLS
Subtly bring up the topic of wish lists with your friends and family months in advance to figure out that unique gift.

GROUP GIFT-MAKING
Use the power of numbers to come together on a special group gift, such as a handmade quilt, a tuck box full of goodies or a scrapbook of memories and pictures.

GIVE A NEW SKILL
Put your gift to good use by teaching a new skill, such as canning or carpentry, that lines up with someone's interests.

WISH LIST CARDS
Make a pretty wish-list card for a loved one to fill out and give back to you.

RECIPE BOOK
Compile your favourite recipes in a hand-bound book for your friends.

BUY

PRETTY PAPER
Keep a horde of beautiful paper lying around to craft a unique card and immediately personalize any gift.

PARTY SUPPLIES
Create a party on the fly with a few spools of streamers, bags o' balloons and glitter – all to make someone's birthday or holiday time extra special.

SOCIALLY CONSCIOUS ENTERTAINMENT

READ

GOOD
good.is
A news website that covers topical and obscure stories from a useful, positive angle.

SHAKE HANDS WITH THE DEVIL
romeodallaire.com
A heart-wrenching and at times gruesome tale from Lieutenant General Romeo Daillaire about his experience peacekeeping in the Rwandan genocide.

JANE GOODALL: THE WOMAN WHO REDEFINED MAN
janegoodall.ca
The wonderfully written and detailed account of humanitarian and scientist Jane Goodall's life mission to revolutionize the study of chimpanzees.

KNOW YOUR RIGHTS
cbc.ca/knowyourrights/ thefineprint
This edifying CBC radio show explores all the angles of Canadians' rights and freedom, with input from lawyers, professors and other guest commentators.

DEMOCRACY NOW
democracynow.org
This daily radio show broadcasts international stories on social movements and issues from around the world.

PROTEST SINGERS
Listen to the great protest singers of yesteryear (Phil Ochs, Joan Baez and Bob Marley) as well as today (Ani DiFranco, John Legend, Michael Franti and Spearhead).

RSA ANIMATE
thersa.org
These amazing illustrated videos are a treat to watch, plus they clearly lay out the ideas and thoughts from some of the leading thinkers of the day: Sir Ken Robinson, Professor Philip Zimbardo and others.

HOT DOCS
hotdocs.ca
Even though the spring film fest is based in Toronto, you can find a listing of all its most recent socially conscious film fare on its website. Hot Docs regularly puts on "Best Of" festivals in various Canadian cities too.

NATIONAL FILM BOARD OF CANADA
nfb.ca
Canada's public producer funds a wealth of documentary and animated film projects.

PLAY

CLIMATE CHALLENGE
bbc.co.uk/sn/hottopics/ climatechange/climate_ challenge/
In this game you are the head of the European Union Nations and forced to navigate the tricky world of climate change policy, while retaining public approval and working around financial restrictions.

THIRD WORLD FARMER
3rdworldfarmer.com
In this interactive game, you are a farmer in a developing country, facing challenges that affect poor farmers every day: crop failures, roving militias, poor education and limited opportunities.
*Not suitable for children.

DARFUR IS DYING
darfurisdying.com
Become a character in a refugee camp in Darfur, where you are forced to battle drought, famine and the constant threat of violence.
*Not suitable for children.

CITY
GUIDE

CANADA VARIES AS MUCH COAST TO COAST AS PARALLEL TO PARALLEL, but living a *me* to *we* lifestyle is possible in every hamlet, town and city. With this guide to local initiatives, organizations, restaurants and shops, you can get started on your living *me* to *we* mission. But we also offer our City Guide recommendations with a disclaimer: this is by no means an exhaustive list – it's only the beginning. Go to the Living Me to We forum at www.metowe.com where you can log in to our cross-Canada, user-generated listings and contribute your own tips for great stores, restaurants and organizations in your area.

BEAUTY & FASHION

BRITISH COLUMBIA

SPOOL OF THREAD
spoolofthread.com
101-649 E. 15th Avenue,
Vancouver.
This bright, homey sewing lounge
in Vancouver offers workshops on
making your own pillowcases or
hawking the retro fabric to sew
them.

TWIGG & HOTTIE
twiggandhottie.com
3671 Main Street, Vancouver.
This cutting-edge shop sells
such socially conscious finds as
compostable, organic shopping
bags and reworked vintage
pieces.

NOT JUST PRETTY
notjustpretty.com
1036 Fort Street, Victoria.
A socially conscious boutique
in Victoria with organic and
sustainable designs from local
creators.

DELUXE JUNK
deluxejunkco.tumblr.com
310 West Cordova Street,
Vancouver.
Known for its amazing selection,
Deluxe Junk also holds the title
of Vancouver's oldest vintage
shop. With reusing and recycling
in mind, the store offers an
easy consignment system for
customers to trade old clothes
for new.

THE PRAIRIES

EDIT SHOPPE
editshoppe.ca
Ethical boutique and online shop
selling great togs in Lethbridge,
Alberta.

EDEN ESSENTIALS
edenessentials.net
Selling out of Calgary's farmers'
market, Eden offers natural
beauty products from West
Coast companies such as Rocky
Mountain Soap Company and
others.

RIVA'S ECO STORE
rivasecostore.com
1237 9th Avenue, Calgary.
Selling all forms of eco-friendly
products, from skincare to
mattresses to building supplies, in
downtown Calgary.

ROCKY MOUNTAIN SOAP
rockymountainsoap.com
This West Coast company makes
delicious soap and a long line
of other natural products, from
deodorant to shampoo. Located
in Winnipeg (1485 Portage
Avenue), Calgary (TD Square),
Edmonton (West Edmonton Mall)
and other locations.

ONTARIO

THE WORKROOM
theworkroom.ca
1340 Queen Street West, Toronto.
This west Toronto hive of
craftiness rents out sewing
machines at $7 an hour, while
regulars are chock-a-block with
helpful tips.

THE SEWING STUDIO
lovesewing.com
1225 Yonge Street, Toronto.
This downtown Toronto studio
offers a range of sewing classes
as well as courses such as "Copy
Your Clothes" that teach you
to mimic the design of your
favourite item of clothing.

PANACEA
panaceaecoshop.com
588 Bloor Street West, Toronto.
This Toronto shop deals in all
organic and eco-friendly goods,
from clothing to personal care.

KNIT CAFÉ
theknitcafetoronto.com
1050 Queen Street West, Toronto.
A friendly little knitting store with
plenty of community courses and
public drop-in nights.

THIEVES
thieves.ca
1156 Queen Street West, Toronto.
Ethical haute couture is yours to
be had at this trendy Queen West
store.

THE BIG CARROT
thebigcarrot.ca
348 Danforth Avenue, Toronto.
This is ground zero for ethical
clothing and food, but its
pharmacy and beauty shop is
also the most extensive in the
city.

PLANET BOTANIX
planetbotanix.com
301 Bank Street, Ottawa.
Plenty of hand-made and natural
cosmetics and personal care
products are sold at this earth-
friendly Ottawa store.

WORKSHOP STUDIO
workshopboutique.ca
242 1/2 Dalhousie Street, Ottawa.
An adorable Ottawa shop that
specializes in hand-made gear
and accessories.

THE MAKE DEN
themakeden.blogspot.com
1207 Bloor Street West, Toronto. Located underneath Bloor West vintage store 69 Vintage Collective, this sewing studio hosts regular clothing-making sessions.

QUEBEC

SMART DESIGN MART
smartdesignmart.blogspot.com
A blog that hosts regular design fairs in Montreal selling the work of talented local crafts people, fashion designers and artists.

EMELINE AND ANNABELLE COUTURE CAFÉ
emelineandannabelle.com
6050, Avenue de Monkland, Montreal.
A quaint little sewing café complete with classes and by-the-hour Bernina machines.

ETHIK BOUTIQUE
ethik-bgc.ca
6050, Rue St-Hubert, Montreal.
A chic boutique dedicated to ethical fashion and sustainable entrepreneurship, with work from 35 designers and 18 countries worldwide.

MARITIMES

GUIDE TO LESS TOXIC PRODUCTS
lesstoxicguide.ca
This Maritime-focused guide rates local cosmetic and personal care products.

KREATIVE KNITS
kreativeknits.yolasite.com
Run by textile and hand-knitting artist Liona Jollota, this yarn shop sells original wool designs made by the owner herself.

THIS CLOTHESHORSE
1530 Queen Street, Halifax.
This small boutique is one of a line of vintage shops along Halifax's Queen Street, all selling local goods and vintage wear.

HALIFAX FARMERS' MARKETS
halifaxfarmersmarket.com
1209 Marginal Road, Pier 20.
You'll find the swank new Farmers' Market down at the historic Pier 20, where dozens of artisans sell hand-made crafts and ethical cosmetics and personal-care products.

FOOD

BRITISH COLUMBIA

THE NAAM CAFÉ
thenaam.com
2724 West Fourth Avenue, Vancouver.
Established n 1968, Vancouver's oldest natural foods restaurant serves vegetarian food with fresh ingredients such as free-range eggs, organic Yukon Gold potatoes and maple syrup. The miso gravy is almost famous.

FARMERS' MARKETS
eatlocal.org
Mingle with local farmers and choose food less-travelled, by shopping at one of the six major markets located in Vancouver. The one in the parking lot of the Kitsilano Community Centre is a local favourite and comes with

bicycle valet parking.

LA TAQUERIA
lataqueria.ca
322 West Hastings, Vancouver. Located in Vancouver's Gastown district, this small restaurant's tacos are made from traditional recipes with local, organic and sustainably produced ingredients, and vegan as well as vegetarian options.

KICKING HORSE COFFEE
kickinghorsecoffee.com
491 Arrow Road, Invermere. Named after a treacherous pass in the Canadian Rockies, this roastery (with a bricks-and-mortar café deep in the heart of the Rockies of Invermere) offers some seriously good beans that are also fair-trade and organic.

THE FOUNDATION
2301 Main Street, Vancouver. Delicious vegan and vegetarian food, inspirational quotes on the wall and affordable prices make this a popular food joint in East Van.

WESTSIDE POCKET MARKET
kitshouse.org
2305 – 2325 West 7th Avenue, Vancouver. Buying local, organic fruit and vegetables is not always the most affordable option. The Kits Neighbourhood House and the Society Promoting Environmental Conservation put on special markets around town, where low-income families can get vouchers for healthy, nutritious food.

THE PRAIRIES

PLANET ORGANIC
planetorganic.ca
With four locations across Edmonton and Calgary, this mega organic supermarket sells lots of tempting groceries.

MONDRAGON
mondragon.ca
91 Albert Street, Winnipeg.
Winnipeg's long-running anarchist bookshop-cum-café is collectively run and serves great ethical fare.

NATURE'S BEST MARKET
2214 14th Avenue, Regina.
Regina's best grocery store selling organic products and produce.

OLD STRATHCONA FARMERS' MARKET
osfm.ca
10130-83 Avenue, Edmonton.
Just off the hip Whyte Ave in Edmonton sits the historic Strathcona Market, selling fresh, local fruit, vegetables and crafts every Saturday.

ORGANIC PLANET WORKERS' CO-OP
organicplanet.coop/wp
877 Westminister Avenue, Winnipeg.
Join this Winnipeg workers' co-op for your hook-up to organic, local and fairly traded produce and products.

ALBERTA FARMERS' MARKETS
sunnygirl.ca
Check out a complete index of farmers' markets across Alberta at this government-run listing.

ONTARIO

SWEET GRASS BISTRO
sweetgrassbistro.ca
108 Murray Street, Ottawa.
This unique restaurant in Ottawa's Byward Market serves up aboriginal fare using all seasonal produce. It's delicious and informative on native traditions and food.

FARMERS' MARKETS
farmersmarketsontario.com
Stop in to one of over 150 markets across Ontario: Toronto favourites include the St. Lawrence Market and the City Hall market at Nathan Phillips Square.

THE BIG CARROT
thebigcarrot.ca
348 Danforth Avenue, Toronto.
This emporium of local, organic and ethical food market is an absolutely essential spot for Toronto east-enders.

WILD ORGANIC WAY
wowrawcafe.ca
22 Carden Street, Guelph.
A Guelph café that serves organic, vegan and raw foods well.

ST. JOHN'S BAKERY
stjohnsbakery.com
153 Broadview Avenue, Toronto.
This bakery sells organic loaves made by participants who take its six-month training program.

MAMA EARTH ORGANICS
mamaearth.ca
Home delivery service of organic food boxes in the Toronto area.

QUEBEC

AUX VIVRES
auxvivres.com
4631 Boulevard Saint-Laurent, Montreal.
Known for fun all-vegan dishes and produce, this restaurant located in the heart of plateau in Montreal serves a vegan poutine you don't need to be vegan to crave.

EQUITA
equita.ca
Check out this Montreal line of fair-trade certified coffee, chocolate, spice, sugar, rice and dried fruits. Its site includes extensive listings for its retailers across Quebec, Ontario, the Maritimes and Manitoba.

LA BRIGADE VOLANTE
brigadevolante.com
1414 Notre Dame Ouest, Montreal.
A catering company turned brunch restaurant uses fresh fruits, lean cuts of meat and all organic, locally and ethically sourced products.

ASSOCIATION DES MARCHES PUBLICS DU QUEBEC
ampq.ca
There are over 100 farmers' markets across the province that sell locally grown and produced fruits, veggies, flowers, fish, bread and more. Check out this association for a listing near you.

MARITIMES

HEARTWOOD VEGETARIAN CUISINE
heartwoodbakerycafe.ca
6250 Quinpool Road, Halifax.

This Halifax mainstay takes healthy eating to a whole new level with delicious cabob desserts and avocados in (almost) everything.

HALIFAX SEAPORT FARMERS' MARKET
halifaxfarmersmarket.com
Halifax's year-round market sure has everyone else beat on location, right by Pier 21 and the Atlantic Ocean.

CALACTUS CAFÉ
125 Church Street, Moncton. As New Brunswick's only completely vegetarian restaurant, this spot serves delicious hand-made flatbreads, massive salads and spicy tofu.

PETE'S FROOTIQUE
petesfrootique.com
Pricy, but quality organic grocery stores in the downtown Halifax area. This place is totally DOES (dangerous on empty stomach). 1515 Dresden Row, Halifax. 1595 Bedford Highway, Bedformd.

BOYCE MARKET
frederictonfarmersmarket.ca
Pick up fresh fiddleheads and local blueberries every Saturday at this long-running farmers' market in downtown Fredericton. 665 George Street, Fredericton.

JUST US! COFFEE ROASTERS CO-OP
justuscoffee.com
A Nova Scotia-based worker-owned roaster that sells environmentally and socially responsible beans, tea and chocolate. There are four cafés across the province: Wolfville, Grand Pre and two in Halifax.

TRANSPORTATION

BRITISH COLUMBIA

CAR FREE VANCOUVER
carfreevancouver.org
This car-free celebration and street festival happens June 20 in five mainland communities in Vancouver.

VANCOUVER AREA CYCLING COALITION
vacc.bc.ca
This cyclists' organization offers workshops on safe cycling skills, incident checklists and popular bike routes in the area.

VANCOUVER URBAN ADVENTURES
vancouverurbanadventures.com
Take a guided walking tour through the Gastown Historic District or a bike tour through Stanley Park with an experienced local guide.

THE PRAIRIES

E-BIKES
e-bikes.ca
This purveyor of e-bikes sells suped-up wheels in Saskatoon, Regina and Lethbridge, Alberta.

EXCHANGE DISTRICT WALKING TOURS
exchangedistrict.org
Take one of the many tours of Winnipeg's historical downtown, each tailored to interests such as architecture, history or sustainable living.

EDMONTON BICYCLE COMMUTERS
edmontonbikes.ca
10047 80th Avenue, Edmonton. With loads of resources online for Edmontonian cyclists, this non-profit community group offers open repair workshops.

ONTARIO

PEDESTRIAN SUNDAYS
pskensington.ca
Toronto's Pedestrian Sundays closes down streets in Kensington Market and other downtown streets to cars on the last Sunday of every month from May to October with an all-day street festival.

TORONTO CYCLISTS UNION
bikeunion.to
This cycling advocacy group keeps track of local issues affecting bike commuters, while also offering help and information on cycling in the city.

BIKE SAUCE
bikesauce.org
235 Broadview Avenue. A co-op bike collective in Toronto's east end where you can repair your own two wheels or ask for help and advice from the volunteers on hand.

BIXI
capital.bixi.com
toronto.bixi.com
Available in both Toronto and Ottawa, this bike sharing system operates with the help of docking stations for picking up bikes in a hurry.

QUEBEC

BIXI
montreal.bixi.com
This popular bike-sharing system in Montreal has taken off across the country with locations in Toronto, Ottawa and another set to arrive in Vancouver. This is a great alternative for getting around in the warmer months.

RIGHT TO MOVE
rtm-lvl.org
1500 de Maisonneuve Ouest, Suite 204, Montreal.
This non-profit cycling organization, started by Concordia students in the late '90s, aims to make biking accessible to everyone through do-it-yourself bike-repair sessions, workshops and recycling and refurbishing bicycles set for the dump. Also, the site has an extensive listing of bicycle resources around Montreal.

MARITIMES

CYCLESMITH
cyclesmith.ca
6122 Quinpool Road, Halifax.
This popular Halifax cycle shop has a great selection of new bikes, free classified ads for used bikes and many handy how-to sessions on the website.

CARSHAREHFX
carsharehfx.ca
Join this car-sharing service that has 12 pick-up points across downtown Halifax and neighbouring Dartmouth.

HALIFAX CYCLING COALITION
cyclehalifax.ca
Check out this site's extensive listings of all local resources, from trail maps to cycling groups to bike blogs.

HOME

CROSS-CANADA GUIDE

HOME DEPOT
homedepot.ca
Check out Home Depot's extensive cross-country listings of government rebates and incentives for home improvement, energy-efficient upgrades.

BRITISH COLUMBIA

LIVESMART BC PROGRAM
livesmartbc.ca
The BC government offers $150 rebates on pre- and post-renovation audits of your home. There are also tax exemptions for select energy-efficient equipment and materials.

BRIGHT IDEAS LOAN
vancity.com/Loans/BrightIdeas
After you've completed your rebated energy audit above, get a low-interest loan, from $3,500 to $20,000, on energy-saving renovations from Van City Bank.

BC HYDRO ENERGY SAVINGS KIT
bchydro.com
If you're a BC Hydro customer and qualify as a low-income household, you can receive a free energy savings kit with CFL lighting, weather stripping, fridge and freezer thermometers and a low-flow shower head.

THE PRAIRIES

CLIMATE CHANGE CENTRAL
climatechangecentral.com
Check out this site for cross-Alberta listings of discounts and rebates on central air conditioning upgrades to Energy Star-qualified appliances and more.

SASKENERGY
saskenergy.com
Rebates for Saskatchewan dwellers include those on programmable thermostats, solar-water systems, natural-gas appliances and other upgrades.

GREEN PLANET HOMES
greenplanethomes.ca
Building a home in the prairies? This construction company builds straw-bale homes and sells milk-based paints, getting back to the pioneer basics.

ONTARIO

ENERGY SAVINGS
energy.gov.on.ca
Check out the Government of Ontario's Ministry of Energy page for a listing for province-city- and town-specific rebates on everything from improved toilets to programmable thermostats.

ENBRIDGE HOME WEATHERIZATION RETROFIT PROGRAM

energy.greenventure.ca/ enbridge-home-weatherization- retrofit-program
Enbridge will shoulder the costs of inspecting, insulating and draft-proofing a customer's home as well as offer tips on cutting costs on your energy bill. Check out the website to see if you qualify.

QUEBEC

ENERGY AUDIT
aee.gouv.qc.ca
If you qualify as a low-income household, you can receive energy-efficient upgrades (such as caulking or weather-stripping windows) and a programmable thermostat.

RENOCLIMAT
aee.gouv.qc.ca/en/my-home/ renoclimat
This home energy-efficiency program certifies homes and offers suggestions for improved upgrades. Renoclimat-certified homes, on average, save up to 25% off their heating bills. There's financial assistance available for those who make the upgrade.

COOP LA MAISON VERT
cooplamaisonverte.com
The first environmental co-op of its kind, this Montreal org sells everything from green cleaning supplies to houseware products to composting toilets.

MARITIMES

EFFICIENCY NS
efficiencyns.ca

This home efficiency program in Nova Scotia offers old appliance recycling options, energy-saving tips and rebates on solar air and water heating, among other offers.

EFFICIENCY NB
efficiencynb.ca
This government program provides financial incentives for making energy efficient upgrades to homes as well as information sessions and tips for conserving energy.

PEI ENERGY EFFICIENT UPGRADE
gov.pe.ca/oee
Islanders can get up to 15% off energy-efficient upgrades to their homes, on anything from programmable thermostats to low-flow toilets.

TAKE CHARGE
takechargenl.ca
This Newfoundland and Labrador program offer rebates per square foot of insulation on basements and attics as well as on money back on upgraded programmable thermostats.

COMMUNITY

BRITISH COLUMBIA

GOVOLUNTEER
govolunteer.ca
A volunteer posting board for British Columbia and Alberta.

BC WOMEN'S MILK BANK
bcwomens.ca
The B.C. Women's Health Centre

and Hospital has operated the country's only milk bank for over 30 years, where women can give or receive breast milk.

QUINTESSENCE FOUNDATION
babyfriendly.ca
This org focuses on promoting the value of donating human breast milk, with workshops, conferences and even breast-feeding challenges that usually take place on the first Saturday of October.

CUTS FOR CANCERS
cutsforcancer.ca
The Canadian Cancer Society hosts an annual hair-cutting event through UBC's Cancer Association. Every year, students gather to give hair for wigs or to cut hair in solidarity for cancer victims.

MOSAIC – WORKPLACE CONNECTIONS
mosaicbc.com/volunteer/ workplace-connections
Through a four-month program with a mentor, this BC-based org helps new immigrants prepare for work in Canada.

THE PRAIRIES

CALGARY REGION IMMIGRANT EMPLOYMENT COUNCIL (CRIEC)
criec.ca
This organization aims to help the influx of immigrants heading into Calgary for work, by pairing up business and community leaders with skilled immigrants in need of work.

HARVEST MOON SOCIETY
harvestmoonsociety.org

This group is focused on linking urban and rural communities in Manitoba through agriculture. Volunteers are welcome year-round to take part or host workshops, or during its festival and celebration of local agriculture.

READ SASKATOON
readsaskatoon.com
This volunteer literacy organization offers volunteer opportunities in both a one-on-one adult training sessions and group family sessions.

ONTARIO

HOMESHARE
cottagedreams.org
Donate your cottage to someone who has recently recovered from cancer treatment.

TORONTO REGION IMMIGRANT EMPLOYMENT COUNCIL (TRIEC)
triec.ca
170 Bloor Street West, Toronto. This organization offers volunteer opportunities to help immigrants coming into the city, by setting up mentor partnerships between new arrivals and established Canadian professionals. The org has offices in York and Peel regions, too.

CULTURELINK
culturelink.ca
2340 Dundas Street West, Toronto.
This immigrant settlement organization offers language sessions, mentorship services and hosts plenty of events in the Toronto area. Volunteers welcome!

OTTAWA COMMUNITY IMMIGRANT SERVICES ORGANIZATION
ociso.org
Multiple locations across Ottawa. This org runs a specialized Career Mentoring Program that pairs up internationally educated professionals with volunteers in the same field.

YMCA
ymcaimmigrantservices.ca
The Kitchener-Waterloo branch of the YMCA offers extensive immigrant settlement services, including mentorship opportunities that match new arrivals with professionals of a similar background.

RYERSON UNIVERSITY TRI-MENTORING PROGRAM
ryerson.ca/studentservices/trimentoring
This program organizes mentorship partnerships between more experienced students and newbies, as well as advising and assistance programs for first-generation students.

MARITIMES

IMMIGRANT SETTLEMENT AND INTEGRATION SERVICES
isisns.ca
This organization has a professional mentorship program for recent immigrants to Nova Scotia.

ECOLOGY ACTION CENTRE
ecologyaction.ca
This activist organization advocates around a variety of sustainable development issues, such as supporting a healthy fishing industry and local food options. This org also hosts workshops on canning and cooking local food.

PARENTING

BRITISH COLUMBIA

ISLAND PARENT
islandparent.ca
Check out this helpful parenting mag, tailored to Vancouver Island families, which includes helpful sections on picking out the perfect educational fit for your children, family events and more.

SAFE TEEN
safeteen.ca
306 East 24th Street, Vancouver. Check out this long-running org that provides anti-bullying workshops for adults and youth.

POWER OF HOPE
powerofhope.org
1921 Fernwood Road, Victoria, British Columbia.
A youth empowerment camp that uses art-centered, experiential and non-traditional learning settings to inspire kids.

YOUNG NATURALISTS CLUB OF BC
ync.ca
1620 Mount Seymour Road, North Vancouver. This non-profit inspires a healthy respect for nature by getting kids out exploring natural areas.

THE PRAIRIES

CENTRE FOR FAMILY LITERACY
famlit.ca
Come visit this family literacy organization that offers adult tutoring, book-reading sessions for babies and reading workshops for kids.

HAPPY NAPPY
townlife.com
Check out this cross-national cloth diaper laundry service that provides service in Edmonton, Calgary, Saskatchewan (as well as BC and Ontario).

ONTARIO

A PEEK INSIDE THE FISHBOWL
quietfish.com
A fun parenting blog from writer Andrea Tomkins, who writes about cool things to do around Ottawa, parenting dilemmas and more.

BUNCHLAND
bunchfamily.ca
A Toronto-based blog that runs kid-friendly events in the city, such as day-time dance parties, secret speakeasy-themed meet-ups and more. (Events are now being offered in Vancouver as well!)

BABY ON THE HIP
babyonthehip.ca
969 Queen Street East/786 College Street, Toronto. A baby-supplies store that sells organic, ethical products and hosts workshops on diapering and infant CPR.

RIVERDALE FARM
friendsofriverdalefarm.com
201 Winchester Street, Toronto. Come visit the pigs, sheep, goats and horses at this wonderful downtown farm – it's free for all and a great day trip for young kids.

QUEBEC

MONTREAL INSECTARIUM
ville.montreal.qc.ca/insectarium
4581 Sherbrooke East, Montreal. A fun and educational place to pass a day with the kids.

WASHABLE DIAPER SERVICE
babyauric.com
Rather than purchasing disposable diapers, you can sign up to this hospital-grade laundering service that delivers diapers right to your door.

LA MAISONNETTE DES PARENTS
maisonnettedesparents.org
6551 St. Laurent Boulevard, Montreal. This holistic parenting centre offers a variety of beneficial services to newly arrived immigrants, neighbouring and troubled families, as well as regular activity programming, seminars, day camps and more.

MARITIMES

MUSEUM OF NATURAL HISTORY
museum.gov.ns.ca/mnhnew
1747 Summer Street, Halifax. Visit the kid-friendly nature exhibits, get outside on a museum-hosted nature walk or visit with Gus, the 88-year-old resident tortoise.

HRM PARENT
hrmparent.ca
A blog and online guide for Halifax parents that comes with a handy directory of educational, community and service links for the city.

URBAN FARM MUSEUM OF SPRYFIELD
urbanfarmspryfield.com
70 Rockingstone Road, Spryfield. This beautiful urban farm is a rustic spot just outside of Halifax, where families can come to garden, help with local food events, share knowledge or just escape from the city.

WORK

BRITISH COLUMBIA

FREE GEEK VANCOUVER
freegeekvancouver.org
Get rid of your electronic waste at this non-profit, which will put it to good use, refurbishing, recycling or using the equipment to provide skills, education and free Internet to the community.

IREPAIR
irepair.ca
Two locations in Vancouver and one in Victoria. There's still hope for your broken and out-of-warranty iPhone at this low-cost Mac repair spot that helps you fix your electronics cheaply.

RETURN IT
return-it.ca
Find out where to recycle your end-of-life electronics through the Return It program, affiliated

with the Electronic Stewardship Association of British Columbia.

THE PRAIRIES

ALBERTA RECYCLING
albertarecycling.ca
Find your nearest collection point for paint, tires and old electronics on this handy directory site.

SARCAN
sarcsarcan.ca
This association operates electronic recycling across Saskatchewan – check here for the depot closest to you.

GREEN MANITOBA
greenmanitoba.ca
The province runs 28 collection depots across the province, all listed on this operating agency's website.

ONTARIO

FREE COMPUTER PICK UP
freerecycling.ca
For Toronto city dwellers, you can schedule a free computer pick up with Free Recycling, a computer recycling program that guarantees your electronics don't end up in the dump.

RECYCLE YOUR ELECTRONICS
recycleyourelectronics.ca
Since you've already paid for the recycling as part of your appliance's price tag, you may as well check out this province-wide website of drop-off locations for those end-of-life electronics.

IREPAIR
irepair.ca
There's still hope for your broken and out-of-warranty iPhone at this low-cost Mac repair spot that helps you fix your electronics cheaply. Two locations in Toronto with two more drop-off repair places in Oakville and Lindsay, Ontario.

MARITIMES

READY SET RECYCLE
readysetrecycle.ca
This Maritime organization works to divert cell phones, laser cartridges, rechargeable batteries and small electronics from ending up in landfills. You can host a drop-off location or use their drop-off locations in grocery stores, hospitals and many other sites across Nova Scotia, New Brunswick and PEI.

ACES
acestewardship.ca
The Atlantic Canada Electronic Stewardship responsibly recycles electronics in Nova Scotia and Prince Edward Island – check the website for more information on what to bring and where to drop it off.

MONEY

BRITISH COLUMBIA

VANCITY
vancity.com
One of the most progressive banks in the country, Vancity offers a line of green banking solutions, such as eco-efficiency loans for retrofits and upgrades to your home, and socially responsible investments that meet ESG criteria (environmental, social and governance).

FREE GEEK VANCOUVER
freegeekvancouver.org
This non-profit accepts computers and nearly all computer-related materials (from cables to keyboards to mice) that are refurbished or recycled in order to provide skills and education, free Internet access and free (or low-cost) computers to the public.

CAMPBELL RIVER BOTTLE DEPOT
powerofhope.org
A youth empowerment camp that uses art-centered, experiential and non-traditional learning settings to inspire kids. 1921 Fernwood Road, Victoria, British Columbia.

ONTARIO

DONATE GOODS
sketch.ca
csbe.net
diabetes.ca
furniturebank.org
Check out Toronto organization Sketch, which helps at-risk youth through art, that is in need of non-monetary donations, such as printing paper, power tools, paint, canvas and first-aid supplies. You can donate old textbooks (Canadian School Book Exchange) as well as gently used pillows, bedding, footwear, kitchen ware and more (Clothesline Program run through

Canadian Diabetes Association) and furniture (via the Furniture Bank).

HELPING WITH FURNITURE
helpingwithfurniture.org
This Ottawa organization picks up gently used furniture donations and delivers everything from living room sets to bedside tables to newly arrived refugee and immigrant families.

QUEBEC

DESJARDINS
fondsdesjardins.com
This prominent Quebec bank offers a line of socially responsible investments and also works with companies to improve their environmental and social practices. Also available in both Ontario and Manitoba.

ENTERTAINMENT

BRITISH COLUMBIA

RAINYCITY DOGS
raincitydogs.com
An online forum for Vancouver dog owners who share information on nearby dog parks, dog walkers and care facilities.

PACIFIC ASSISTANCE DOG RESCUE
pads.ca
This volunteer-run organization places companion dogs with people who have disabilities. Volunteers can work directly with the dogs (raising, dog-sitting, training, kennel care or simply

just cuddling!) or take on jobs in the office, maintenance or education programs.

VICTORIA ADOPTABLES
victoriaadoptables.com
Listings of cats, kittens, dogs, puppies and bunnies up for adoption in the Victoria, Vancouver Island and Gulf Island communities.

THE TYEE
thetyee.ca
A great, online British Columbia-based magazine that runs alternative stories on social issues, book reviews, politics and more.

ONE OF A KIND SHOW
oneofakindvancouver.com
Just in time for holiday shopping, this massive festival of handmade crafts that takes place early December, is the perfect place to pick up a locally made, unique gift.

OPEN CINEMA
opencinema.ca
Check out this socially conscious Vancouver Island cinema that screens films with a message.

THE PRAIRIES

MANDOLIN BOOKS
mandolinbooks.com
A coffee shop and purveyor of used books, great for an afternoon break.

MENDEL ART GALLERY
mendel.ca
Check out the Saskatoon art gallery that is ground zero for culture in the city and hosts many

fun family workshops and events. 950 Spadina Crescent East, Saskatoon.

ONTARIO

TORONTO CAT RESCUE
torontocatrescue.ca
This non-profit, no-kill, volunteer-run cat adoption organization doesn't have a physical shelter, but uses a network of rotating foster homes to take care of its litter. It is always in need of loving owners or short-term volunteers to take cats on limited-time foster basis.

LOCALLY YOURS
locallyyours.ca
In the deep south of Ontario, this gift company sources local food products (wine jelly, handmade soap and baskets) from the Windsor and Essex county region into one handy gift basket.

HOT DOCS FILM FESTIVAL
hotdocs.ca
506 Bloor Street West, Toronto. Every spring, this film festival screens over 150 docs from Canada and around the world. Recently, the festival acquired the iconic Bloor Cinema to host more cutting-edge film festivals year round.

ONE OF A KIND SHOW
oneofakindshow.com/toronto
Just in time for holiday shopping, this massive festival of handmade crafts is the perfect source for a locally made and unique gift.

SNAKES AND LATTES
snakesandlattes.com
600 Bloor Street West, Toronto. Toronto's first board-game café

has over 1,500 different games to try out. Bring the whole family for some bonding time.

BEEHIVE CRAFT COLLECTIVE
beehivecraftcollective.ca
This Hamilton-based craft collection holds a summer craft fair and has lots of links to local and Canadian artisans.

DOORS OPEN TORONTO
toronto.ca/doorsopen
See a whole new side of this city by taking part in this once-a-year throwing open of churches, art deco treatment plants, private firms and the rooftops of hotels for an entire weekend in late May.

ST. LAWRENCE MARKET
stlawrencemarket.com
Open throughout the week, this historic downtown market holds a special farmers' market on Saturdays and an antiques fair on Sunday. 92 Front Street East, Toronto.

QUEBEC

CASA DEL POPOLO
casadelpopolo.com
4848 St. Laurent, Montreal.
This café, music space and bar is a community gathering point for Montreal's Mile End area.

DRAWN & QUARTERLY
drawnandquarterly.com
A home-grown comics publishing company that hosts regular readings and events, and has a great selection of graphic novels and other literature.

PIN PALS BLOG
thepinpals.typepad.com

Check out this crafty Montreal team's blog for regular DIY projects and craft-fair listings happening around town.

LES TAM-TAMS DU MONT-ROYAL
Parc du Mont-Royal.
A regular Sunday affair that brings together different communities at Mont Royal Park, some to play Loorping games, others to sell wares, others simply to dance or hang out on the grassy knoll.

MARITIMES

HALIFAX GARDEN NETWORK
museum.gov.ns.ca/mnhnew
1747 Summer Street, Halifax.
Visit the kid-friendly nature exhibits, get outside on a museum-hosted nature walk or visit with Gus, the 88-year-old resident tortoise.

JOHN W. DOULL BOOKSTORE
doullbooks.com
1684 Barrington Street, Halifax
A true adventure in book buying, this shop on Barrington Street in downtown Halifax has towering stacks of used and antiquarian books for sale.

THE COAST
thecoast.ca
Support Halifax's thriving arts and culture scene by finding out about community events in the local alt-weekly paper.

TRIDENT BOOKSELLERS AND CAFÉ
tridenthalifax.com
1256 Hollis Street, Halifax.
A quaint little Halifax café in the

city's south end that roasts its own beans and sells used books.

BRITISH COLUMBIA

VANCOUVER ISLANDS, GULF ISLANDS
bcferries.com
Hop on a ferry to the Vancouver and Gulf Islands, sans vehicle, and you'll save money, get exercise and can island hop from Salt Spring to Gabriola, exploring old growth trees and beautiful coasts.

MOUNTAIN BIKING BC
mountainbikingbc.ca
Check out this site for regional guides to biking across British Columbia as well as a directory to events and trails.

THE PRAIRIES

THE PAS
thepasarea.com
Few venture so far north in Canada, but the beautiful Pas region, some 600 kms northwest of Winnipeg, has history and adventure to its name. This is the spot where French and English trappers once traded with native tribes, with many heritage points in the area, as well as Clearwater Lake Provincial Park, renowned for its clean, clear and cool water.

THE ROCKIES
canadianrockies.net
Take a day trip to the National Parks of Banff or Jasper. Moraine Lake is a beautiful blue glacial

lake, often restricted by the regular grizzly bear sightings in the area, has a beautiful view that was featured on a 1960s and 1970s version of the Canadian $20 bill. If you want to take in a completely different side of Alberta, you could visit the oil sands of Fort McMurray on a tour.

CALGARY IS AWESOME
calgaryisawesome.com
Rediscover your city with this fun city blog and its many event listings. Or, if you're visiting the city for the first time, seek this online spot out for some guidance to local events.

ONTARIO

THE THOUSANDS ISLANDS
visit1000islands.com
boldtcastle.com
1000islandsplayhouse.com
The Thousand Islands area near Kingston, Ontario is a great locals' getaway. There's the beautiful island castle of Boldt and the 1000 Islands Playhouse (in Gananoque) among the many islands to explore.

ONTARIO CULINARY TOURISM
ontarioculinary.com
Use this website to find all the resources you need for a tasty road trip through Ontario's wine and culinary regions.

PLANET TRAVELER, TORONTO
Stay at the greenest hotel in North America, with its LEED Platinum Certification, which uses geothermal temperature control,

motion sensor LED lights, solar and photo voltaic panels and water-reclamation techniques.

PARKBUS
parkbus.ca
Don't have a car but still want to camp? ParkBus operates express bus service between Toronto, Algonquin and Killarney Provincial Parks, with service for backpackers and canoers.

BIKETRAIN
biketrain.ca
A cycle tourism initiative that links up downtown Toronto types with bike trails in the Niagara wine and tourist region, Windsor and Essex county – all with a quick hop on the VIA Rail, GO Train or Bike Bus offered by the Northland Bike Bus.

ME TO WE STORE
metowe.com
223 Carlton Street, Toronto. Come down to the Me to We Store to plan your ethical vacation abroad.

QUEBEC

EASTERN TOWNSHIPS
www.easterntownships.org
At the southern end of Quebec lies the Eastern Townships with its sizable English-speaking population, wine routes and a veritable foodie playground. Take a cycling tour, visit a spa or hike through the wilderness in between meals featuring some of the best Canadian food.

THE LAURENTIANS
www.laurentians.com
Only an hour north of Montreal, this region, with its string of

mountains, massive forests and 9,000 rivers and lakes, is the perfect day or weekend escape to nature.

ALT HOTELS
www.althotels.ca
This line of hotels in Montreal and Brossard (and another soon to open at Toronto's Pearson Airport) focuses on providing a cheap, but still eco-conscious alternative to an overnight stay.

ROUTE VERTE
www.routeverte.com
This visionary bike network has over 4,000 km of paths across the province. There is also a coordinated network of B&Bs, camping sites and rest areas that offer special menus for cyclists, repair and pump stations as well as information on bicycle stores and sites in the nearby area.

Acknowledgements

THIS BOOK ITSELF IS AN ACT OF LIVING *ME* TO *WE*. Using the knowledge and collective effort of so many extraordinary individuals, we created a guide that truly reflects Canada and the world we live in. We were supported by so many dedicated people who helped map out our ideas into a practical guide for everyday living.

We cannot express sufficient thanks and praise to researcher and project manager Laura Trethewey for her dedication and passion in living the message of this book. Laura spent countless hours researching tips, conducting and compiling interviews, and handling all the details to make the dream of this book a reality. Her commitment kept us going through long nights and many drafts, and for everything she has done we are incredibly grateful. Laura thanks her family for their help, support and love: Dad, Mom, Karen, Kristin, Thelma and George Trethewey, and Stan Prest. As well, thanks to her friends for their support and encouragement: Ashley Scarlett, Chloe Ellingson, Lola Landekevic, Ashleigh Gaul, Nick Hutcheson, Steve Kwok and Bridgid Young.

Without Shelley Page, this book would not be as witty, thoughtful and thorough as it is. We cannot thank you enough for reading through every idea, calling in for brainstorm sessions, giving feedback so generously and supporting us as we wrote out page after page. We are forever in your debt for the time and dedication you brought to this project. We continue to be inspired by your gargantuan efforts to raise Me to We books to a higher level of substance and inspiration.

Heartfelt gratitude is due to Frances Data for pulling together such a sleek and beautiful layout for our guide. Your keen eye for clarity as well as beauty turned this book into the wonderful-looking book it is today. Thank you also to Marisa Antonello and her creative team at TurnStyle Imaging for their energy poured into the cover and illustrations that truly brought *Living Me to We* to life. Your keen eye and truly creative mind shaped these illustrations. Special thanks is also due to our talented team of consultants: Doug O'Neill, Ed Gillis, Sharon McAuley and Theresa Kielburger. Thank you for reading through successive drafts of *Living Me to We*. We couldn't have asked for a more committed and talented team to share our writing with.

Thank you to the writers at Me to We and Free The Children who looked through many early drafts, offering yours skills and guidance along the way: Ryan Bolton, who brought the book to fruition, Sapna Goel, who oversaw the talented team that worked on the book, Henry Claflin, Shannon D'Arcy, Drew Davidson, Katie Hewitt, Olga Kidisevic, Rebecca McAllister, Kari Trogen, Peter Goffin, Sean Deasy and Genevieve Westrope.

So many team members across both Free The Children and Me to We offered help, whether that was passing along a helpful book or sending an introductory email, we thank you: Laura Roantree, Hannah Feldberg, Janice Sousa, Shauna Rhodes, David Johnson, Tara Skjodt, Anil Phulesar, Marc Henry, Don Lane, Amelie Dinh, James Cooper, Alec Bozzo, Andrew Ventura, Alex Apostol, Mihee Kim, Dana Dignard, Kim Plewes, Sarah Aquilina, Marianne Woods, Brittany Russell, Kelly Creeden, Beth Campbell, Rachael Quick, Leysa Cerswell and Angelique de Montbrun. As well, thank you to the talented photographers on the team who brought such vivid imagery to this book: Michael Rajzman, Josh Sam and Sara Cornthwaite.

Thank you to Victor Li at Free The Children for his patience in explaining all the ins and outs of donating wisely to charity. Thank you to Angie Gurley, Tamara Kaftalovich and the PR team for their vision in linking this book with its readers.

Thank you to the activists, philanthropists, singers, writers, musicians and notable Canadians who contributed personal stories: Margaret Atwood, Jian Ghomeshi, Rick Hansen, Anne Murray, Michaëlle Jean, Seamus O'Regan, Sam Roberts, George Stroumboulopoulos, Duncan and Jonnie Penn, Ben Nemtin and Dave Lingwood of *The Buried Life* as well as Ed Robertson, Jim Creeggan, Kevin Hearn and Tyler Stewart of The Barenaked Ladies.

We are forever grateful to the many people who participated in interviews about their life to demonstrate the power of living *me* to *we*. This book would not be possible without you! Thank you to Jennifer Atkinson, Dennis Carlsen, Drew Davidson, Keith Ferrazzi, the Girouard family, Patricia Green, Carole Hochu, Laura Hamilton, Corinne Impey, David Johnson, Rob Klea, Sylvia Kleindinst, Angelisa Lake, Francois Langlois, Jason Martorino, Kamal Mattar, Meghan McKiernan, Shelley Page, Bob Papadopoulos, Rory Sinclair, Amy Swanton, Jordan Banks, Charlotte Empey, Evan Solomon and Sunshine Wilson.

This book was years in the making and along the way we asked the advice of many talented individuals. Thank you to Chris Winter at We Conserve, May Ho Stepanek at Plant a Row, Grow a Row, Jane Farrow at Jane's Walk, Kate Munroe at CMHC, Jen at the Otesha Project, Cameron Chalmers at Community Services in the District of Squamish, to Carole Hochu and Mandy Parerra at the Ontario Electronic Stewardship, to Rebecca Spring at Retire your Ride, to Eugene Ellmen and Sarah Thomson at the Social Investment Organization, Yen To at RBC, Sucheta Rajagopal at Hampton Securities, Austin Mardon, Alison Cousland at CAAMP, Joanna M. Dwyer at Toronto Habitat for Humanity, to Debbie and Karyn at the Workroom, Paul Hess at the University of Toronto, Natalie Purschwitz, Rowena Hopkins at NS Farmers Markets, Mary Forstbauer at B.C. Farmers Markets, Kate Rusnak at Terrachoice, Dion Oxford at The Gateway, Danielle Buklis and Susan Antler at the Composting Council of Canada, Eileen Kotowich, Heather Garrod, Paul Hughes, Carmel Sabourin, Arlene Pastor, Kathryn Borel, Derek Flack, David Topping, Jessica Roelink, Kirti Mukri, Carmel Sabourin, Elizabeth Varma, Emily Wright and many, many more.

Thank you to Sara Smith and Eusis Dougan-McKenzie from Jantzi-Sustainalytics for sharing their expertise in the field of ethical investment. We couldn't have created excellent chapters on money without your guidance and insight. Thank you to Mary Beth Menzies at Green Tech Services and Bob Papadopoulos at Red Brick Inspections for their invaluable help conducting an energy audit and explaining how a home retrofit works. Thank you to Lindsey Coulter, the Queen of Green at the David Suzuki Foundation, for sharing her knowledge on home-made beauty products. Thank you to the talented, fun and always professional team at CP24 and CTV: Leila Siu, Darren Weir, Perry St. Germaine, Jeremy Burgess and Brian Carr. You heard us out on these ideas, helped create an archive of video interviews and found us many of the amazing individuals and organizations featured in this book.

Me to We is grateful to the dedicated team at Douglas & McIntyre and Greystone Books. A special thank you to Scott McIntyre, Rob Sanders, Richard Nadeau, Susan Rana, Carra Simpson and the whole team.

Thank you to all of our media partners who have supported socially conscious living. These include the wonderful people at Bell Media's CTV and CP24, *Metro News*, *Toronto Life* and *Canadian Living*. We would like to express special thanks to the team at the *Globe and Mail*, including Jill Borra, John Stackhouse, Phillip Crawley and Sue Grimbly. Thank you to the *Vancouver Sun*, *Winnipeg Free Press*, *Toronto Star*, *Victoria Times Colonist*, *Calgary Herald*, *Waterloo Record*, *Halifax Chronicle Herald* and the *Huffington Post*.

We also remain thankful for the support of Michelle Douglas, Eva Haller, Greg Rogers and the Toronto Catholic District School Board; Dr. Chris Spence and the Toronto District School Board; Jacki Kelley and the incredible team at Universal McCann; Chris and Tania Carnegie; Don and Debbie Morrison; Bill Thomas and everyone at KPMG; Lorne Segal; David Aisenstat and The Keg Steakhouse & Bar; Nicole Rustad and the team at Club Penguin; David Baum; Hartley Richardson; Mark Chipman; Bob Silver; Susanne Boyce; Mia Farrow; Holly Branson; Michael Stone; the Aquilini Family; Rene Malo; Jeff Skoll and Jim Berk and everyone at Participant Media; the

Battat family; John and Dorothea Gaither; Jonathan White; the Caldwell Family; Della and Stuart McLaughlin and everyone at Grouse Mountain; the cast of *Degrassi*; Leonard Kurz; the Longo family; Jennifer Tory; Cynthia Keysey; Anne Klamar; Jason Saul; the Church family; Dayle Haddon; the Hopper-Dean family; the Heimark family; the Shapanksy family and Tony Hauser.

Much appreciation to our corporate and organizational partners, especially the teams at National Bank Financial Group, OMERS Worldwide, Investors Group; Air Canada Kids Horizons; EF Canada; Telus; the Martin Aboriginal Education Initiative; the Djavad Mowafaghian Foundation; Nelson Education; Pareto; RBC; Research in Motion; the Skoll Foundation; Torys LLP; Virgin Atlantic; Facebook Canada; Pattison One Stop; the Stillman Family Foundation; Medecis; B. Toys; the J. W. McConnell Family Foundation; Artbound; the Michael "Pinball" Clemons Foundation; AOL Canada; Teck Resources and Nature's Path Organic.

Thanks to Roxanne Joyal for her years of partnership and support.

Love to our Mimi, who remains our biggest fan.

We would not be where we are today without the love and support of our parents, Fred and Theresa. Thanks for everything, Mom and Dad!

CRAIG & MARC KIELBURGER

ABOUT FREE THE CHILDREN

FREE THE CHILDREN
children helping children through education

Free The Children is the world's largest network of children helping children through education, with more than one million youth involved in our innovative education and development programs in 45 countries. Founded in 1995 by international child rights activist Craig Kielburger, we are a charity and educational partner that believes in a world where all young people are free to achieve their fullest potential as agents of change. Our domestic programs educate, engage and empower hundreds of thousands of youth in North America, the UK and around the world. Our international projects have brought over 650 schools and school rooms to youth and provided clean water, health care and sanitation to one million people around the world.

Visit **www.freethechildren.com** to find out more.

ABOUT ME TO WE

me to we

Better choices for a better world

Me to We is an innovative social enterprise that provides people with better choices for a better world. Through socially conscious and environmentally friendly products and life-changing experiences, Me to We measures the bottom line, not by dollars earned, but by the number of lives we change and the positive social and environmental impact we make. In addition, half of Me to We's net profit is donated to Free The Children and the other half is reinvested to grow the enterprise.

Visit **www.metowe.com** to find out more.

BRING A SPEAKER TO YOUR SCHOOL

Bring a speaker to your child's school, your parent and educator association or your workplace conferences—and take away all you need to "be the change."

The team at Me to We has traveled the world to discover the most inspirational people with remarkable stories and life experiences. From community activists to former child soldiers to social entrepreneurs, our roster of energetic, experienced speakers are leading the Me to We movement: living and working in developing communities, helping businesses achieve social responsibility and inspiring auditoriums of youth and educators to action.

They leave audiences with a desire to take action and make a difference. They'll make you laugh, cry and gain new perspective on what really matters. Be warned: their passion is contagious!

Visit **www.metowe.com/speakers** to learn more.

JOIN US ON A ME TO WE TRIP

If you want to really experience another culture and truly see the world, take a Me to We trip. Sure, you could lounge on yet another beach, surrounded by other stressed-out visitors seeing the usual tourist traps. But why not seek out a volunteer travel experience that radically changes your perspective, positively transforming the lives of others?

Our staff live and work in the communities you'll visit, coordinating schoolbuilding and supporting development in participation with local communities. On a Me to We trip, you'll learn leadership skills, experience new cultures and forge truly meaningful connections.

Over 3,000 adventurous people of all ages have chosen to volunteer abroad with us. You'll do incredible things, like build schools and assist on clean water projects. You'll meet exuberant children excited at new possibilities for learning, and be immersed in local communities.

You'll get your hands dirty digging wells and laying foundations. But you'll love it. You'll come home with a sunburn—and the biggest smile you've ever had on your face. And best of all, you'll have memories that last a lifetime.

Visit **www.metowe.com/trips** to learn more.

READ BOOKS WITH A REAL MESSAGE

Standing Tall
Spencer West

Navigating life on his hands, Spencer has always lived with purpose. But living in a world where society seems to dictate happiness, Spencer wanted more out of life than just a paycheck and material possessions. He wanted to have an impact, but wasn't always sure how. That was until he had the epiphany that being different was for a reason. This is the candid, coming-of-age story of a young man's journey of working hard, laughing a lot and always standing tall.

The World Needs Your Kid
Craig and Marc Kielburger and Shelley Page

This unique guide to parenting is centered on a simple but profound philosophy that will encourage children to become global citizens. Drawing on life lessons from such remarkable individuals as Jane Goodall, Elie Wiesel and Archbishop Desmond Tutu, award-winning journalist Shelley Page and Craig and Marc Kielburger demonstrate how small actions make huge differences in the life of a child and can ultimately change the world.

Free the Children
Craig Kielburger

This is the story that launched a movement. *Free the Children* recounts 12-year-old Craig Kielburger's remarkable odyssey across South Asia, meeting some of the world's most disadvantaged children, exploring slums and sweatshops and fighting to rescue children from the chains of inhumane conditions.

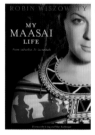

My Maasai Life
Robin Wiszowaty

In her early 20s, Robin Wiszowaty left the ordinary world behind to join a traditional Maasai family. In the sweeping vistas and dusty footpaths of rural Kenya, she embraced a way of life unlike she'd ever known. With full-colour photographs from her adventures, Robin's heart-wrenching story will inspire you to question your own definitions of home, happiness and family.

Take Action! A Guide to Active Citizenship
Craig and Marc Kielburger

Want to begin changing the world? *Take Action!* is a vivid, hands-on guide to active citizenship packed with the tools young people need to make a difference. Accomplished human rights activists Craig and Marc Kielburger share valuable tips and advice from their experiences as founders of Free The Children and the Me to We movement. Ideal for grades 8–10, *Take Action!* shows that young people don't need to wait to be the leaders of tomorrow—this journey begins now.

Take More Action: How to Change the World
Craig and Marc Kielburger with Deepa Shankaran

Ready to take the next step? *Take More Action* is our advanced guide to global citizenship, empowering young people to be world-changers – around the world or in their own backyard. Brilliantly illustrated and packed with powerful quotes, stories and resources, *Take More Action* includes invaluable material on character education, ethical leadership, effective activism and global citizenship. Ideal for Grades 10 and up, *Take More Action* paves the way for a lifetime of social action.

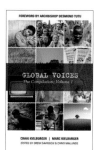

Me to We
Craig and Marc Kielburger

Me to We is a manual, a manifesto and a movement. It's a philosophy that is both timeless and revolutionary. It's about finding meaning in our lives and our world by reaching out to others – by thinking *we* instead of *me*. In this book, Craig and Marc Kielburger share the knowledge they have gained through living lives of service. Their own reflections and ideas are complimented and reinforced by contributors like Richard Gere, Dr. Jane Goodall, Kim Phuc, Her Majesty Queen Noor, Arch Bishop Desmond Tutu and Oprah Winfrey.

Global Voices, The Compilation: Vol. 1
Craig and Marc Kielburger

Global Voices aims to tell the untold stories of people and issues from around the world. With a foreword from Archbishop Desmond Tutu and discussion questions to help spark debate, this book will inspire young readers to deepen their understanding of issues and explore how they can change these headlines. Tied together from Craig and Marc's columns that have appeared in newspapers across Canada, *Global Voices* touches on the tough issues in an enlightening, enjoyable read.

Lessons from a Street Kid
Craig Kielburger

After starting Free The Children when he was 12-years-old, Craig Kielburger continued his crusade in Brazil. It was on the streets of Salvador, Brazil that Craig learned the firsthand stories of street children. In this easy-to-read, full-colour illustrated children's book, the reader learns about the joys of these very children. Follow the adventure perfect for young readers that defies borders in the universal act of generosity.

My Maasai Life: A Child's Adventure in Kenya
Robin Wiszowaty

Follow a young Robin Wiszowaty as she travels to Kenya for the first time. Living with the Maasai people, Robin explores the land with her new family. Getting water, finding wood and singing songs. And don't forget the zebras, cows and giraffes. It is all a part of the adventure with the Maasai. With Robin as a guide, the full-colour illustrations only enhance any child's own adventure into the world of the Maasai.

Visit **www.metowe.com/books** to see our full list of bestselling books.

The Buy a Book, Give a Book promise ensures that for every Me to We book purchased, a notebook will be given to a child in a developing country.

Stay up-to-date with living *me* to *we*:

 twitter.com/craigkielburger

 facebook.com/craigkielburger

Go to **www.metowe.com** to connect with other Canadians that are passionate about social change. Find your own cause and support for socially conscious living.